Sinatra
The Untold Story

Sinatra
The Untold Story

Michael Munn

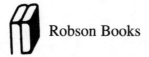 Robson Books

First published in Great Britain in 2001 by
Robson Books,
64 Brewery Road, London N7 9NY

A member of the Chrysalis Group plc

British Library Cataloguing in Publication Data
A catalogue record for this title is available from the British
Library.

ISBN 1 86105 366 5

Typeset in Times by FiSH Books, London WC1.
Printed and bound in Great Britain by Butler & Tanner Ltd.,
London and Frome

For
Maureen and Alan

Contents

Introduction

This is not a full-scale biography of Frank Sinatra. There have simply been enough of those. Rather, this is a book about something very few people ever knew about the man, and, for reasons I shall explain, I became one of those few.

In writing this, I hope at long last to be able to put into perspective much of what has gone down as innuendo, speculation and rumour as far as his dealings with the Mafia and the Kennedys were concerned. In doing so I hope to reveal a secret part of Sinatra's life that will give the reader an insight into why he did what he did, how he did it, and why, in the end, he could never come clean and, in his lifetime, do away with all that innuendo, speculation and rumour.

I'm laying my cards on the table. I was never a great fan of Frank Sinatra, so I'm not compelled by some sense of loyalty or sheer awe to paint a rose-tinted portrait of the man. I was a child of the late sixties, and so I was never into Sinatra's music. I got to know Sinatra on screen long before I ever started taking notice of him as a singer. As a kid, I discovered him as a movie actor when I saw *Von Ryan's Express*. I managed to catch him in a revival of *Sergeants Three* and, when I was a little older, I admired him greatly in *The Detective*. I caught some of his older dramatic films, like *The Man with the Golden Arm* and *The Joker is Wild*, on television. He always struck me as an accomplished and engaging actor, and he gave performances in films like *The Manchurian Candidate* and, of course, *From Here to Eternity* to prove it.

I didn't care much for his old musicals, which I only saw on television. I just am not a fan of musicals per se. However, I did catch a brief revival of *High Society* at a cinema, and it remains the only musical of his that I really like, and is one of the few musicals for which I bothered to buy the soundtrack album. Through that album, I began to appreciate Sinatra more as a singer, but it didn't compel me to go out and buy all his records. I can appreciate the magic of some of his recordings, however, particularly 'Strangers in the Night', 'My Way' and 'New York, New York', so Sinatra fans may not consider me a complete Philistine. I even ended up buying a double album of his greatest hits, but that and the *High Society* soundtrack are the only recordings of his that I possess.

In more recent years, I have come to appreciate the magic of Frank Sinatra the entertainer through old television clips of him performing, because in those clips I can see just why he became such a legend. In fact, before writing this book, I actively sought anything on television that showed him in concert, and when I came across a documentary entitled *The Rat Pack*, I found myself drawn to those sections devoted to the shows the Rat Pack put on at the Sands Hotel at the time they were making *Ocean's Eleven*. Seeing those, you can't help but wish you'd been there to see it all in person. (Incidentally, the title *Ocean's Eleven* is sometimes written as *Ocean's 11*, but to me it looks like a film in a long series of sequels, so I shall stick to *Ocean's Eleven*.)

For me, the fascination of Sinatra came from my friendship with Ava Gardner and the tales she told me about their affair, their marriage and their ongoing friendship. I also learned a great deal about how his associations with the Mafia affected their relationship, and she told me stories of her own, sometimes frightening, encounters with mobsters that have never been published before. Those stories put a whole new spin on the couple's already strained affair and marriage, not to mention their attempts at reconciliation. From Ava I learned about the nuts and bolts of the man. What I was to learn from some of her friends – who were also those who had been among the closest to Sinatra – was a bonus. It was an education I never sought, but it proved to be the beginning of a fascination I still have about the relationship between Hollywood and crime: not because I am interested in crime, but because I wanted to learn all I could about Hollywood history. Crime – organised crime – played a big part in that. Somewhere at the centre of it all was Frank Sinatra.

As I have written in depth on the subject in previous books, it has been continually frustrating for me not to be able to tell the whole truth. Sinatra would not have approved of that. Despite all the evidence of his relations with the Mafia, he had publicly denied them too many times for him ever to backtrack. In fact, he denied them to the very end. Yet what comes out of this story is not a picture of a man who was somehow evil because of his Mob associations, but a picture of a man who, in his own way, did something that was inherently heroic, if, perhaps, foolhardy.

Over the years I have had the opportunity to meet and interview many of the old Hollywood 'greats' and, because of the rather unique knowledge I had of Sinatra, care of Ava and the others, I was able to ask very pointed questions and get some of these other stars to talk about Frank in relation to what has now become the subject of this book.

I always thought that one day I would write a full-scale biography of him and include all the material I'd been saving up, but, as I have said, that has been done too many times. This, therefore, is a book with a theme that has gone unnoticed by the creators of the many biographies and documentaries about him. I believe I can guarantee that, unless you happen to be one of 'the few' like me, you will discover things about Frank Sinatra you never knew and which have eluded the most meticulous of his biographers.

To have revealed earlier what I now do would also have necessitated revealing my sources, and those sources – like Sinatra himself – would not have been best pleased. Although Ava was the one who insisted I know about everything, it was clear that it was not something I should ever reveal in her lifetime, and especially not in Sinatra's. He made that clear himself, as shall eventually be explained.

Somehow, vicariously, I feel I have got to know Sinatra – or rather, I have got to know more about him than I ever could through reading any of the biographies on him. To know Sinatra is to avoid the contradictions that have created the many myths about the man and, instead, to lay out those 'nuts and bolts' simply, purely and without judgement.

Chapter One

A Call to Madrid

Frank Sinatra was distraught at the news of Marilyn Monroe's death. It was broadcast across the American continent on the morning of Sunday 5 August 1962. Frank's only thought on losing the woman he had not only loved but had intended to marry was to call the other woman he still loved and to whom he had once been married.

As Ava Gardner recalled it, the phone in her villa in Madrid rang sometime during Sunday evening, Spanish time. She was not in a particularly good mood. She was somewhere in the middle of a chaotic schedule to film the Boxer Rebellion epic *55 Days at Peking*, a task that she was finding increasingly unbearable. Sunday had been her day off, and she was depressed at the prospect of going back to work in the morning. She was dissatisfied with the script, which was being rewritten on a daily basis, and she felt trapped in the seemingly never-ending four-month schedule that, to her, consisted largely of concentrating on the heroic deeds of her leading man, Charlton Heston.

Heston had never wanted Ava in the film in the first place, believing she was totally miscast as a Russian countess caught up in the middle of the conflict between Chinese Boxers and the various international legations besieged in old Peking. She had only accepted the part because it was being filmed virtually on her doorstep. She had forsaken the glitz and glamour of Hollywood to settle in Spain, where she enjoyed a number of love affairs with dashing matadors.

This, then, was what was going on in Ava's life and career at the moment she received Frank's call.

Her spirits lifted when she heard his voice. Despite their troubled past, she always loved hearing from him. Yet on this occasion she quickly became concerned by his despondent tone.

'Have you heard the news?' he asked her.

'What news?'

'They found Marilyn dead this morning.'

Ava had not heard the news. For all she knew, the news had not yet been broken in Spain, or anywhere else in Europe. She was not surprised when Sinatra told her the police had said that Monroe had killed herself with an overdose of barbiturates. It was common knowledge that Marilyn had made a number of suicide attempts, troubled as she was by personal and professional setbacks. Nevertheless, the news still shocked Ava.

She made some remark to Sinatra to the effect that everybody knew Marilyn was going to succeed in one of her suicide attempts one day.

What Sinatra then said stunned her into momentary silence. 'I'm not so sure she killed herself.'

She remembered being unable to speak, and hardly daring to ask the question, but finally she said, 'What do you think happened?'

Sinatra said he couldn't be sure, but he strongly suspected that Monroe had been murdered.

'You can't be serious,' she told him.

He was – and he had a strong hunch who was behind it. When she asked him who he thought was responsible, he said, 'My phone may be bugged. I've said more than I should. I need to see you.'

Ava explained that she couldn't get away because she was stuck in Spain making 'that interminable picture'. At that he exploded and accused her of never being there for him when he needed her. That was one of the problems in their marriage. Ava recalled that they were both self-centred people, but he was always far more demanding and explosive than she was. That was not the only thing that had caused their legendary rift. She said she never hated him, but there was much about him – mainly to do with his Mafia associations – that she truly despised. Despite all that, she said, there was still much about him that she loved. In fact, she never stopped loving him, and according to those who knew – and they included John Huston and Sammy Davis Jr – he still loved her. Sinatra was a man capable of loving more than one woman at a time. That had also been a problem in their marriage – not that Ava was exactly a chaste woman, as she admitted.

She didn't like the accusation he made of her not being there for him when he needed her, but she also recognised that he was completely distraught and in a severe state of shock. This was one time when she didn't allow her own temperament to rise to the bait. She tried to make him understand that she could not just abandon the film – as much as she would have liked to – and suggested that he come to her.

He was also tied down to commitments, however, and getting out of the country was impossible for him. Ava promised to meet with him as soon as she could. She somehow managed to soothe his anger, and, when he had calmed down, she asked, 'The person you suspect: is it someone I know?'

He told her it was best he didn't say on the phone. He was going to instigate a private investigation of his own into Marilyn's death.

'Be careful,' she warned him.

'I swear, I'm going to kill the fucking son-of-a-bitch myself,' he responded.

She recognised that kind of talk. She knew that he was perfectly capable of dealing out retribution. He was a man who had lived in the shadow of the Mafia all his life, and some of his closest business associates were among the most prominent men in the Mob.

She once told me, 'You couldn't be married to Frank and not know he was also married to the Mob.'

He seemed to think he was somehow invincible because of that. She had always hated his Mob associations. She recalled a time when they were at a nightclub and were joined uninvited at their table by a 'hood', who seemed impervious to the glare Ava gave him. A photographer spotted the celebrity couple, walked over and took a picture of them. Ava very calmly got up, took the camera away from the photographer, opened it up and pulled out the film. Then she handed the camera back to the photographer, who, obviously thinking better of having an argument about it, wandered away. The last thing Ava wanted was to find herself and Frank pictured in the newspaper with a mobster. In fact, she was surprised that Frank had not already decked the photographer. She was sure he would have done if she hadn't been so quick to act herself.

She had often told Frank that she hated having 'those fucking hoods' around him all the time, but he always tried to reassure her that they were just people he happened to know because of the business he was in. The fact was, just about every entertainer who worked their way up through the clubs would have had contact with mobsters, because most of those clubs were run by the Mob. What had really alarmed Ava, however, was knowing that, following their divorce, Frank had gone into a full-scale partnership with just about the biggest mafioso of all – Sam Giancana.

Sinatra's great pride and joy was the Cal-Neva Lodge, a hotel and casino on the border of California and Nevada of which he had become part-owner. The hotel was on the California side of the border, the casino just inside Nevada. Although Sinatra always denied it publicly, Sam Giancana was his silent partner in the business.

Peter Lawford, once one of Sinatra's closest friends and, for a while, one of MGM's major stars, told me in an interview in 1974, 'Frank thought Giancana was the king. I don't want to say too much about it, but it was because of his association with Giancana that Frank and I fell out, and I don't want to say too much about that either.' (In due course, Lawford would privately relate the full story, and I was to learn a very different version of events from that which has gone down as documented history in regard to Sinatra and his alleged associations with both Giancana and John F Kennedy. I also came to learn why Lawford had been prepared to go along with the myth that became generally regarded as fact. But more of that later.)

Lawford continued, 'I'll tell you this: when Frank sang "My Kind of Town Chicago Is", it was his tribute to Giancana. But I detested Giancana, who was an awful guy with a gargoyle face and weasel nose. I couldn't stand him, but Frank idolised him.'

Ava later recalled, 'It's funny, but when Frank told me he had a hunch about who killed Marilyn, my first thought was Sam Giancana.' During the phone call Frank made to her on 5 August 1962, she had had to stop herself blurting out Giancana's name – just in case, as Sinatra feared, his phone was being bugged. All she could say to him was, 'If you're thinking of who I'm thinking of, leave it alone.' She knew that, if Giancana was the man Frank suspected, then he was putting himself in grave danger by even thinking of accusing the Chicago Mob boss of Monroe's murder.

'You don't have to worry about me,' Sinatra assured Ava.

'But I do.'

After that phone call, Ava became ever more restless and disturbed, and it showed in her behaviour on the set of *55 Days at Peking*. In fact, she ended up working only three months on the film because she became so temperamental and difficult – which to

Heston was sheer unprofessional behaviour – that in one particular scene many of her lines were given to Paul Lucas, and her character was quickly killed off in a hastily written extra scene.

Although she didn't know for sure that Frank had been referring to Sam Giancana, Ava knew for certain that, regardless of whether or not he was behind the death of Marilyn Monroe, he was certainly perfectly capable of having Frank killed. As events would prove, she was right to be afraid.

Frank Sinatra and Sam Giancana, once the best of friends and business associates, would become deadly rivals in a vendetta that, until now, has been kept well and truly under wraps. How I came to find out about it is part of this story. Here, for the first time, is the untold story behind the vendetta Frank Sinatra himself instigated – a vendetta that would threaten his own life and lead to the gradual decline of the most powerful Mafia boss of his time.

Chapter Two

Born in the Shadow of the Mafia

To tell you what I want to tell you, it is important to understand what Frank Sinatra's association with the Mafia was all about – and why he was linked to it. It is also vital to understand the Mafia itself.

Publicly, Sinatra always denied any involvement. Considering the stigma that comes with such an association, not to mention the consequences, who can blame him? He was never what you would call 'a member' of the Mafia. He was no 'wise guy' or 'goodfella'. Yet he was involved as an entertainer and as a business associate in legitimate enterprises – although the lines drawn between legitimate and nefarious at times became a little blurred. The implications made by many who have written or spoken about him suggest that he had to be a criminal, a gangster, a hood – that he was just as bad as those in the Mob with whom he worked. Others have been less harsh, but have still criticised him for his dealings with the Mafia.

Many feel Frank Sinatra had only himself to blame for his involvement in the Mafia and the strife it would cause him in later years. Many have been judge and jury over his associations with organised crime. So much has been written and spoken about his life, with so many contradictory reports, that it

sometimes becomes a crusade for researchers, authors and
journalists to attempt to unravel the truth behind the myth. The
man was complex, no doubt. Perhaps because of his com-
plexities, people who knew him gave differing accounts from
their own subjective viewpoints that only added to the confusion
and so created the many myths. I think it is fair to state that his
character was almost that of a split personality. That's just the
way he was. Nonetheless, there was change in him over the years,
coloured at first by his association with the Mafia and then by his
dissociation *from* the Mafia.

Sinatra was loved by some, hated by others, and he lived by a
code that demanded respect – usually earned through friendship,
sometimes earned through fear. Of himself, he demanded charity
where he felt it was due. There was no doubt Sinatra was
generous, a virtue that became stronger than his vices in his latter
years. Yet to those who got on the wrong side of him, he was a
demon and for them none of the countless charitable acts he did
could ever turn him into a saint.

For me, there is no great mystery behind the many faces of
Frank Sinatra. It is a very simple equation. He was merely a
product of his environment, and of his genes. That is why I don't
feel Sinatra can be wholly blamed for his Mob associations. Yet
at the same time he was obviously accountable for some of his
choices that landed him in trouble later in life. There was to come
a time when he would turn the corner and seek some kind of
redemption from it all, But from the very beginning he was not
in a position to avoid the Mafia.

Frank Sinatra was born under the alarmingly growing shadow of
the Mafia on 19 December 1915, in the centre of what was
known as Little Italy in Hoboken, across the Hudson Bay from
Manhattan. His Sicilian grandparents had migrated to America
after the birth of Frank's father, Anthony Martin, who became

known to his family and friends as Marty. Marty was raised in a tough neighbourhood where Sicilians and Italians were considered to be of a lower class than the German and Irish immigrants. It was important for someone like Marty to learn to take care of himself, and he would later become a prizefighter when his son Frank was still a boy.

Frank's mother was Natalie Catherine 'Dolly' Garavente, the daughter of Italian immigrants. It has been said that Dolly was even tougher than Marty. She was also considerably better educated, and at first there was opposition to the union of Marty and Dolly between their respective families. It was almost a Romeo-and-Juliet scenario.

Hoboken became the first city in America to come under the Prohibition law that made the whole of America dry by 1919. It could be argued that President Woodrow Wilson was to blame for the rise in the Mafia's dominance of the underworld in America at that time: Prohibition provided the underworld with the perfect business – providing illegal booze to the millions of thirsty Americans who still wanted to drink liquor. It was a case of supply and demand.

The rise of the Mafia in America can be traced to the beginning of the twentieth century. Sicilian and Italian gangs sprang up all over the United States, usually in the ghettos where Sicilian and Italian immigrants were inevitably housed. New York was probably the city with the most ghettos – for the Italians, the Hungarians, the Irish, the Germans and the Russians. It was inevitable that these ghettos produced their own ethnic gangs, with the general purpose of protecting their own kind. That was the foundation of the Mafia in Sicily. In Italy there were also the Neapolitan Camorra and the Calabrian Carbonari. It was upon these organisations that the Italian and Sicilian immigrants based their own Mafia-style operations.

Despite their criminal activities, the gangs initially had the welfare of their own communities at heart. They might well have remained little more than local gangs with no real power if Prohibition had not been introduced. Supplying illegal liquor was the enterprise that really gave them power and even put the Sicilian gangs into competition with each other. On a localised basis, however, the Mafia gangs were there to help a needy Sicilian or Italian.

It was not difficult for Marty, with his Sicilian ancestry, to find himself employed by the New Jersey Mob as they set up business to provide thirsty Americans with bootleg booze. Marty became a guard on trucks carrying alcohol, while Dolly became the proprietor of a saloon. Frank's parents were part and parcel of the bootleg trade, and the Mafia was behind it. Frank therefore grew up in a family environment where the Mafia was an unavoidable part of everyday life.

Some say – and Frank Sinatra himself promoted the idea – that Marty was not cut out to be a mobster. He was too laid back, and when he got injured in a raid on one of the trucks he was guarding, he quit the bootleg business and became a fireman. Yet he was not such a soft touch. Frank had a favourite story about his father that he told many people. Marty once loaned fifty dollars to a guy who ran a bar. When time came for repayment, the debtor simply said he wasn't going to pay. In his own laid-back way, Marty went outside to where the bar owner's horse was tied up. He brought the horse into the bar, took out a gun, and shot it dead.

Despite this ruthless streak in Marty, who had learned his tough ways from his Mafia friends, Dolly was the more domineering of the couple. She had a temper on her that put young Frank in his place many times. She was probably the only person Frank Sinatra was ever scared of. Yet she was also a caring woman who became influential in the Italian community. She knew local politicians – and she knew the New Jersey Mob boss, Willie Moretti. She would go to court for any non-English-speaking Italians who found themselves under arrest, and she translated for them. She acted as a midwife for those women who couldn't afford proper health care. Despite being a Catholic, she was also available to help out young single women who found themselves pregnant. She was, as Ava put it, 'an abortionist'.

With a ruthless, tough-talking father, a mother whose charitable nature sometimes broke the law, and an upbringing in a neighbourhood where the weak were victims of violence on the streets, Frank was simply a product of his environment and his genes. He was, in a real sense, an amalgamation of Marty and Dolly. Frank may have been a small kid, but he was a kid with attitude. He would never think twice about getting into a fight with anyone who called him a 'wop'.

The links his parents had with the Mafia were not links that could easily be broken, and in those days there seemed to be no reason to break them. The Mafia took care of its own, and the violence that broke out was usually between the Mafia and the Irish gangs who vied for control of the speakeasies of New Jersey. The Mafia came out on top. They were the ones who grew stronger and came to dominate the underworld of America.

It was Dolly who encouraged Frank to become an entertainer. He sang like an angel, and she had ambitions for him. Dolly knew the right person to help: Willie Moretti. By then Prohibition had been repealed, but the Mafia maintained its control over most clubs. Dolly asked Moretti to give sixteen-year-old Frank a job at one of his clubs doing anything, even if it was waiting on tables, if only he could also have the chance to sing a few numbers. Moretti got Frank a job at the Rustic Cabin, but it didn't take long for young Frank to get into an argument with the proprietor, which resulted in a fight. Frank was duly fired.

With Dolly's help, he began singing at Democratic Party conventions, which led to other performances with small bands. He began to grow ambitious, deciding that all he ever wanted to do from then on was to be an entertainer. He also, as Ava noted, wanted to be 'a tough guy'. He was a chip off the old block. Under the circumstances, it was only natural that he should look up to men like Willie Moretti.

Frank Sinatra was not the only entertainer who revered the guys who ruled the roost in the neighbourhood of his youth. James Cagney and Tony Curtis, while of different generations, came from similar backgrounds, and both told me they had known gangsters and admired them. 'They were like Robin Hood and his Merry Men,' Cagney said. 'They were kind to us kids. You could only like them. And anyway, there were only three ways a kid from my neighbourhood could get ahead. You could become a prizefighter, go into show business, or go into crime.' Marty Sinatra had been a prizefighter and, for a time, a gangster. Young Frank had inherited his mother's ambitious streak, and he was going to be an entertainer no matter what – but he was also intent on emulating the gangsters his parents knew.

Plenty of the other kids felt the same about the mobsters. It just so happened that the vast majority of them didn't become famous entertainers like Frank Sinatra. While these mafiosi were looked upon as local heroes, however, it should not be forgotten that these men were, underneath it all, ruthless. Willie Moretti may have had a genuine affection for young Frank and was willing to show him favours, but he was one of a breed of men whose job description included murder.

In those early years, mobsters did not necessarily work as a united front. Organised crime had yet to be organised, and that happened only when Charles 'Lucky' Luciano managed to do away – in typical brutal manner – with the New York Mafia bosses who were over him, until he became the self-proclaimed 'Boss of all Bosses'. It was Luciano who organised crime, and brought all willing gangsters who were not necessarily Sicilian (or even Italian – Meyer Lansky and Benjamin 'Bugsy' Siegel were both Jews) into the Family. That Family was the Mafia.

At the start of Moretti's rise to infamy, he was a partner with Abner 'Longie' Zwillman, and together they ran the rackets in New Jersey. It was Bugsy Siegel who said, 'We only kill ourselves.' His claim, and that of the other mobsters, was that they didn't murder innocent victims. As Arthur Miller's Italian-American lawyer Alfieri said in the play *A View from the Bridge*, 'There were many who were justly shot by unjust men.'

Yet no one could know for sure that Siegel, or any of the other mobsters, never killed innocent victims. The Mafia controlled its various nefarious businesses with fear. Any proprietor of a saloon who refused to stock the Mob's liquor was likely to die in an explosion that blew his premises apart. Union leaders who refused to bend to the whims of the Mob were likely to find themselves falling through windows.

There was also the Mob murder of the movie actress Thelma Todd in 1935. It was one of the Mob's best-kept secrets for years, but many in Hollywood knew that Thelma had been killed on the orders of Lucky Luciano. It seems that Thelma had been brought into the Family by marriage to Luciano's man in Los Angeles, Pasquale 'Pat' DiCicco. It didn't help that she had an affair with Luciano himself, his power over her having been propagated by the drugs on which he happily got her hooked.

When he told her that he wanted to install an illegal casino in her famous Thelma Todd's Roadside Café, she turned him down. The thing is, you never turned down the Mafia – especially not powerful and ruthless men like Luciano. Her biggest mistake, though, was in trying to blow the whistle on him by calling the LA District Attorney's office. Her call was intercepted by someone in the DA's office who was in Luciano's pocket, and so Lucky personally ordered her death.

Her studio boss, Hal Roach, knew – as did many in Hollywood – that Thelma was a victim of the Mob, and when her attorney told Roach that he intended to prove it, Roach prevailed upon him to drop the matter. The lesson Hollywood learned was that the Mafia could easily find excuses for killing anyone who got in their way.

This, then, was how the Mafia worked, and the fact that someone might be a Hollywood movie star did not make them immune from the Mob's own form of retribution.

It was in 1935, the year Thelma Todd was murdered, that Frank Sinatra joined a trio of musicians who became known as The Hoboken Four. They performed on radio in *Major Bowes' Amateur Parade*, and this gave them a modest profile as they toured the States, putting on shows. Leading American band leader Henry James heard Frank sing, and invited him to join his band as vocalist.

With the Henry James Band, Sinatra went to Atlantic City where, through his mother's connections, he came into contact with Paul 'Skinny' Emilio D'Amato, who ran the famous 500 Club. In Atlantic City, Skinny D'Amato was something of a legend. Born there in 1904, he started gambling when he was just ten years old. He organised craps games in empty houses, on street corners and in schoolyards. He made all the money from these games simply because he was the one who owned the cards and the dice. He had an uncle in the Mafia who lent him forty dollars to open up a cigar store. The store was just a front for a pool room and casino in the back rooms. Skinny was only fifteen, but, by the time he was sixteen, he had cigar stores all over town. Some years further down the line, he was running the famous 500 Club – and he was in the employ of the Mafia. That was the way it was in those days. Most of the big clubs were run by the Mob.

One can only speculate that, had Sinatra not been born of parents who had their own connections to the Mafia, he might not, perhaps, have pursued his association with the mobsters. The fact is, however, that his parents did have their connections, and Frank was completely comfortable around those characters. After all, as just about every actor I've spoken to who came into contact with gangsters has told me, those people were – with some exceptions – charming, friendly, and just dying to do you a favour.

It is also a fact that any entertainer who wanted to work in the clubs had to do business with the Mafia, whether they liked it or not. By the early 1950s, the Mob owned just about every major nightclub in the country. Caesar's Palace, the Sahara and the Riviera would be under the control of Chicago; New York's Meyer Lansky, Lucky Luciano's money man, controlled the Thunderbird Club; Moe Daltz of the Cleveland Mob ran the Desert Inn; the Stardust was run jointly by the Cleveland and Californian Mobs (although later Sam Giancana would push his way in to own the biggest share in the club); New York's Frank Costello and Phil Kastel owned the Tropicana; Lansky and Frank Costello managed the Sands Hotel (and would later sell shares to George Raft and Frank Sinatra). Sinatra and D'Amato would later become business associates as part-owners of the Cal-Neva Lodge by Lake Tahoe on the Nevada–California border. Sinatra would, in a very real sense, become a business associate of the Mob, despite his many denials.

In 1940 Tommy Dorsey, arguably America's most popular band leader, invited Sinatra to join his band. There is some argument over *where* Sinatra actually joined Dorsey's band, but that doesn't matter. It was another step up the ladder of success. Singing with Dorsey taught Sinatra a great deal about technique and style.

In 1943 Sinatra and his wife Nancy moved to Hasbrouk Heights, New Jersey, and on Friday nights he would join Willie Moretti and Frank Costello to watch the fights at Madison Square Garden. These were the very people who, according to Joseph 'Doc' Statcher, who answered directly to Meyer Lansky, 'had spent a lot of money helping [Sinatra] in his career, ever since he was with Tommy Dorsey's band'.

Dorsey had given Sinatra a contract that earned Dorsey a considerable amount from everything Sinatra would make for life, from personal appearances to records. The exact amount Dorsey was making from Sinatra is open to argument: some say Sinatra had to hand over a third of all he earned to Dorsey; others put it at half. In 1943, Sinatra attempted to break his contract with Dorsey and they filed suit against each other. Although publicly Sinatra was to deny it, the matter was finally settled out of court by the intervention of Willie Moretti. His men paid Dorsey a visit and basically threatened to break his legs, or even kill him, if he didn't release Sinatra from his contract. Legend has it that Dorsey, terrified at having a gun put to his head, caved in. As Ava told it, however, Dorsey laughed at the hoods and said he would release Sinatra from his contract simply because he was 'sick of him'.

Whether Dorsey gave in through fear or merely because he wanted to be rid of the troublesome singer, the fact was that the Mafia had yet again stepped in to aid Sinatra. With the Mob backing him, Frank felt he was becoming invincible. He didn't seem to consider that being forever in the Mob's debt could be a drawback.

It was around this time that the FBI began making notes about Sinatra's association with the Mob. The irony of it all was that J Edgar Hoover, head of the FBI, publicly declared that there was no such thing as either the Mafia in America, or any kind of organised crime syndicate. The truth was that Hoover was being blackmailed by the Mafia, who had incriminating photographs of him engaged in homosexual activities. Hoover had come up with a set of rules by which all FBI agents had to live. Homosexuality was one of the deadly sins – and yet the Mafia had evidence that Hoover was in actuality 'the Queen of the FBI'. It was not difficult to persuade him to leave the Mob well alone. All the same, Hoover had agents keeping tabs on the Mob, and the reports were strictly for his eyes only.

It came to his attention that Frank Sinatra was more than just an entertainer working in Mob-run clubs. A report was drawn up showing that, in January 1947, Frank was invited by the powerful Fischetti brothers, cousins of Al Capone, to join them in Miami for a few days before flying to Cuba to pay homage to the still-enthroned Boss of all Bosses, Lucky Luciano. Luciano had previously been released from prison and exiled back to Italy after the Second World War – his reward for getting the Mafia to aid the American Navy's secret intelligence in the invasion of Sicily. He was now back as close to American shores as he could get – in Cuba.

Sinatra and the Fischettis stayed at the Miami mansion owned by Luciano on Allison Island. The night before they left for Cuba, Frank put on a free show at the Mob-run casino, the Colonial Inn, in Hallendale. He pulled in a rich crowd which could only lose at the gambling tables.

FBI agents were watching closely the next day, 11 February, as Sinatra and the Fischettis flew to Havana. Rocco Fischetti and Frank both carried attaché cases. According to the FBI report, there was as much as two million dollars in cash in those cases: tribute for the Boss of all Bosses. The agents followed them to the Hotel Nacional, where Luciano lived in a luxurious penthouse suite. Thirty-six other suites had been reserved for his many guests, all of them bringing him tributes in cash.

Sinatra stayed for four days and entertained the biggest mobsters in America, including Albert Anastasia, Willie Moretti, Meyer Lansky, Vito Genovese, Frank Costello and Joe Adonis. When the party was over, Sinatra joined his wife Nancy in Mexico.

Hoover quietly noted the reports made by his agents, and hid them away, presumably for possible future use. He would find these reports a very useful tool when the time came to blackmail his rival for power over the Federal Government, President Jack F Kennedy.

*

By the time Frank had become the idol of the bobbysoxers, he was dressing, according to Jo-Carroll Silvers (former wife of Phil Silvers), 'in a vulgar, showy way [and] like gangsters, he gave great big, crude, showy presents'.

Jo-Carroll remembered a day when she and her husband were having dinner with Sinatra at Chasens when Bugsy Siegel, 'the Hollywood Don', came in and passed their table. Sinatra and Silvers stood and said with reverence, 'Hello, Mr Siegel. How are you?' When they sat down, Sinatra and Silvers talked about how many people Siegel must have killed, and speculated on what might have been his preferred methods of killing. Jo-Carroll recalled 'the awe Frank had in his voice when he talked about Siegel. He wanted to emulate Bugsy.'

One major star in Hollywood was already a student of Siegel – George Raft. Sinatra made a point of getting to know Raft, who, as James Cagney told it, was part of the Mob 'with a capital M'. Originally a dancer and gigolo, Raft become an actor only because it suited the Mob to send him to Hollywood. When his old pal from New York, Benjamin 'Bugsy' Siegel, arrived in Los Angeles to take over the extras' union, as well as setting up various illicit businesses on behalf of the New York Mafia boss Lucky Luciano, George Raft was already there to help him any way he could.

Years later, when Raft had been all but blacklisted by Hollywood for his Mafia connections – and Siegel himself was long in his grave, having been murdered for cheating the Mafia out of millions to build the Flamingo in Las Vegas – Sinatra gave Raft a part in *Ocean's Eleven*. When Bugsy was alive, Raft had been a star. After he was killed, Raft was no longer wanted by the major studios. As he said at the time, 'When they killed Benny, they killed me too.'

For Frank, however, any friend of the late Bugsy Siegel was a friend of his. It was also a way for Frank to pay respect to the

Mob, who had Raft on their payroll as a front man for many of their casinos. Nonetheless, it was the killing of Bugsy Siegel in June 1947 that ultimately put Sinatra in a situation that threatened to reveal his Mob associations and ruin his career for ever.

Lucky Luciano and Meyer Lansky had ordered the death of Bugsy Siegel in the Hollywood home of Siegel's girlfriend, Virginia Hill. They obviously felt, through their blackmail of Hoover, that they would remain immune from any consequences, but the contract killing of a mobster in Hollywood was enough to wake America up to the fact that organised crime did exist. The man who quickly instigated an investigation into the Mafia was Senator Estes Kefauver, who formed a committee before which all known mafiosi were called to testify in front of television cameras in 1950.

Meanwhile, the US State Department put a ban on all legal drug shipments to Cuba unless the government threw Luciano out of the country. Lucky found himself unceremoniously deported back to Italy, and a new Mafia hierarchy was set up in America. Frank Costello became the Boss of Bosses.

Sam Giancana, from Chicago, took control of the Hollywood rackets, which had previously been in the hands of two Chicago gangsters, George Browne and Willie Bioff. They had controlled the International Alliance of Theater Stage Employees – the union that represented personnel such as props men, art directors, cameramen, script supervisors and sound and lab technicians. Their shakedown of Hollywood had begun in 1934 and ended in 1941 when Bioff and Browne were indicted for extorting huge sums from virtually all the major studios.

Sam 'Mooney' Giancana was also known as Doctor Goldberg and, as Sinatra called him, Sam the Cigar. Because Giancana played such an important role in Sinatra's life, and became the eventual target of Frank's personal vendetta, I should explain something about this man who would initially be described by Sinatra as his friend, and later as his enemy.

Sam was in Chicago in the early days when different Mob factions were vying for control of that city and the state of Illinois. In 1924, Johnny Torrio was the boss of Chicago, with many elite killers in his employ, including Al Capone. Capone had visions of greatness, and he decided on taking out Torrio. To do the job he chose sixteen-year-old Sam Giancana and Leonard 'Needles' Gianola. Giancana worked for Diamond Joe Esposito, leader of one of the Chicago gangs. He was called 'Mooney' because he was the craziest, or 'mooniest', of the hoods who worked for Esposito. Yet Giancana held to no loyalty and, recognising that Al Capone was the man most likely to take control of Chicago, had no compulsion in carrying out Capone's orders.

They ambushed Torrio as he was unloading shopping from his car. Although riddled with bullets, Torrio survived and fled to New York, where Charles Luciano permitted Frank Costello to set him up in a little bootlegging. Despite the failure to kill Torrio, Capone was impressed with Giancana and gave him further contracts.

Giancana was careful to make himself available to both Diamond Joe and Capone, and when Capone succeeded in driving Esposito out of town and taking over Chicago, Giancana was one of his favoured enforcers. He was one of the gunmen chosen by Capone to take out seven of the gang run by George 'Bugs' Moran, one of Capone's rivals. The hit occurred on 14 February 1929, and became immortalised in crime annals as the St Valentine's Day Massacre.

When Capone finally went to jail and Frank Nitti took control of Chicago, Sam Giancana was given responsibility for all executions ordered by Nitti. It was in 1946 that Nitti sent Giancana to Hollywood to take control of Chicago's rackets in the movie capital. When Siegel was killed a year later, Giancana's hold on Hollywood grew stronger. He not only took over where Bioff and Browne had left off, but persuaded producers, studios and entertainers to agree to his own style of business, which provided him with a great deal of extortion money as well as a valuable supply of entertainers for his own casinos.

Later in 1947 he handed over the Hollywood reins to Johnny Roselli, who had been Nitti's West Coast representative. He set himself up as an agent, but his main job was to find fading movie stars who needed to get back up again, and to help newcomers up the ladder of success. These people would come to realise that their 'sponsor' was Sam Giancana.

As the Kefauver Committee began their proceedings, Frank Sinatra was shaken when he was summoned to meet lawyer Joseph L Nellis, whose job was to decide if Sinatra should appear before the committee. His whole career suddenly hung in the balance.

Chapter Three

Ava

Women were always one of Sinatra's great weaknesses. He was, from an early age, 'a rampant stud', as Ava put it.

She also said that the trouble with Frank was that he was a truly passionate man, able to love more than one woman at a time. With him, it wasn't just pure lust, it was true affection. Of course, this was not the case with every woman he slept with, but when he fell for a woman, he fell hook, line and sinker. Once in love, he rarely fell out of it, even when he fell in love with another.

In 1934, aged just nineteen, he met and fell for seventeen-year-old Nancy Rose Barbato. They remained lovers for some years, even though, from time to time, Frank would find new conquests. In 1938 he was charged with seducing a girl on the promise of marriage, which was then a serious crime. He was arrested and mug shots were taken, but the girl had to drop the charge when she admitted she was already married.

For Nancy it was a crushing blow, as well as an embarrassing situation in which to find herself. Frank promised her that he would never go with another woman. He also had his mother, Dolly, to contend with. She berated him for his promiscuous nature and in the end virtually bulldozed him into marrying Nancy, thinking that would settle him down.

It didn't. They did have children, however. The first, Nancy, was born in 1940, with little Frankie Jr coming along in 1943. Then came Tina, in 1946.

There were many more women in his life, but none of them had such a devastating effect on his hormones or his heart as Ava Gardner. They met in 1949: he was 34, she 27. They became passionate lovers.

Ava was married to the musician Artie Shaw at the time, and she admitted to me that she never stopped loving Shaw, even while she was falling in love with Frank. 'We were alike in that way,' she said of herself and Frank. 'We could both love each other and still have room in our hearts for others.'

The air of danger that pervaded about Frank excited her. She recalled a wild car ride in the night when he produced a gun and began firing aimlessly out of the window. The wild ride stopped when they were pulled over by a patrolman. The first person he noticed was Ava. 'Ava Gardner!' he exclaimed.

It riled Frank that this cop had not recognised *him* straight away, even though he was peering through the driver's window. Then the patrolman did see that it was Frank Sinatra at the wheel. 'Oh, excuse me, Mr Sinatra,' he said. 'I didn't recognise you at first.'

Ava was smiling her most sensuous smile at the policeman, determined to charm him into letting them go. Frank realised this, and said, 'So, officer, are you going to arrest Ava Gardner?'

'Good God, no,' said the cop. 'I just wondered what you were shooting at. I mean, nobody's after you, are they?'

'No,' said Frank. 'We're quite safe.'

'That's okay then. I mean, when I saw your car and heard the shots, I just thought . . . '

'Sorry if we worried you, officer,' Ava cooed. She was not conceited, but she knew very well that men found her irresistible, and she often used it to her advantage.

'But you really should be careful,' the cop said to Sinatra, even though he was gazing into Ava's gorgeous eyes. 'I mean, be careful with that gun.'

'I will,' said Sinatra. 'Is that all?'

Ava was still mentally seducing the policeman, and he said, 'Yes, I think so.'

'So can we go now?'

'Yes, you can go.'

Off they drove into the night, with Ava laughing and Frank confused by mixed emotions at being let off a possible charge and having to endure the attention Ava had given the cop.

Ava knew that Francis, as she always called him, still loved Nancy, but she insisted that he was not happy in his marriage and, since she wasn't happy in hers, it suited them both to have a wild, passionate and, she maintained, truly loving affair. He became totally besotted with her, and friends noted that he seemed to be going crazy in a way that was damaging his career. He even went as far as calling her up and saying he was going to kill himself. It was all bluff – a way of getting the attention he felt she wasn't truly giving him. Ava began pressuring Frank to divorce Nancy.

Eddie Fisher recalled a time when he and Sinatra were appearing together on *The Eddie Cantor Show*. Sinatra put his arms around Fisher's shoulders, revealing thin cuts on his wrists.

It drove him even crazier when, having divorced Artie Shaw, Ava went to Spain to make *Pandora and the Flying Dutchman* in 1950. There she had an affair with her co-star, a bullfighter called Juan Montalvo, who played her lover in the film. She said that her affair was simply a matter of needing and getting sex and had nothing to do with love: she still loved Frank with a passion. (She went to some lengths to try to explain to me her own code of morality whereby sex should never be confused with love, and, even where there was love, there was still a need for sex – and not necessarily with the one you loved. It was a morality that was, and is, widespread in show business, and Ava was just one of many who lived by it.)

News of Ava's affair tore Sinatra apart. His torment was not helped by the fact that he had become dependent on sleeping tablets, and, when he made an attempt to give them up, he simply drank himself to sleep each night with Jack Daniel's. He had become an emotional wreck, and the effect this had on his physical wellbeing was devastating. He lost weight, and he began to lose his voice, ushering in the beginnings of his career problems.

He decided to fly out to Spain to confront Ava, who was shocked to see how sick he had become. She told me that the truth was, Frank needed her more than she needed him, but he was nevertheless something of an obsession for her, if not as much as she was for him. She simply told him that she was free to sleep with whomever she pleased while he was still married to Nancy. She was treating him in a way no other woman had ever dared to do. It was the way he usually treated other women.

The result was one of their many rows, and she finally told him to leave her alone – unless he divorced Nancy. As far as Frank was concerned, he didn't need to divorce Nancy, who was a Catholic and disapproved of divorce; but he was prepared to leave her to be with Ava. That wasn't good enough for Ava.

Sinatra left Spain and headed for Paris, where, to his utter astonishment, Ava turned up in his hotel room in the middle of the night, and climbed into bed with him. She told me she wanted him to know what he was missing. She was up and gone before he woke up the next morning.

When Ava finished filming, she returned to Los Angeles – and to Frank. They moved into a rented house together. Then she went with him to London, where he performed at the London Palladium, his voice somewhat restored by medication and cups of tea. After that they flew to New York. Nancy, realising she had lost him for ever, resigned herself to a divorce. Ava was delighted. Nonetheless, the pre-divorce settlement was financially crippling for Sinatra, whose career was still sliding downward.

Ava made Frank introduce her to his parents. Dolly liked her, but Marty didn't. Ava said, 'I had Dolly on my side, and she was the powerhouse in the family, so that was all that mattered.'

Frank Sinatra's career in films had seen him hit the highs in the late 1940s at Metro-Goldwyn-Mayer, the studio that made the biggest and best musicals of that era. Frank was in two of MGM's best, *Anchors Aweigh* and *On the Town*, both with Gene Kelly – but what he really wanted was to be taken seriously as a dramatic actor. MGM didn't see it that way, and it led to that studio dropping him in 1950. Sinatra expected his departure from Metro to lead to more challenging films, but it only added to his professional decline.

His first film after Metro was for RKO, a comedy called *Double Dynamite*, and although he was billed as the star, the whole project was really a vehicle for RKO's leading lady, Jane Russell. To add insult to injury, the best comic lines were delivered by Groucho Marx.

Then, in 1951, Universal starred Frank in a programmer called *Meet Danny Wilson*, in which he played a crooner who gets to the top with the help of gangsters. It was all so close to the truth, as his leading lady Shelley Winters noted:

'I believe the film was partly Frank's idea as he had his buddy Don Maguire write it for him. Draw your own conclusions.

'It was a difficult picture to make, not least because it was being done in such a hurry to try and save Mr Sinatra's flagging career. As I understood it, he badly needed the $25,000 Universal was paying him, and so the film was virtually thrown together, like my wardrobe which was not made to fit me but my wardrobe dummy. I had four production numbers to perform with Mr Sinatra and only four days to learn them.

'I remember that we began filming in chaos, mainly because Frank was then in the process of divorcing Nancy so he could marry Ava. I noticed that he had a lot of visits from his two young kids, from priests and psychiatrists. To be fair, everyone was giving him a bad time. Everyone knew of his problems and his affair with Ava, and the industry itself as well as the columnists were giving him a bad time.

'I began filming scared to death of him because I had been told tales about his legendary temper tantrums and also his kindness, so I started the film believing I was working with a Jekyll and Hyde. On the first day of rehearsal, I received a note from him suggesting we rehearse in his dressing room. Well! I thought that could be a mistake as I knew his reputation, and I also knew and liked Nancy – they were still married then. I wanted to make sure we kept our association as professional as possible, and also I happened to be a bigger star at Universal than he was, so I sent him a note back saying that this was my studio and that we would rehearse on the stage, as scheduled.

'Mr Sinatra was upset by that – and I suppose I may have read the signs wrong and that he only wanted to rehearse in the dressing room so we could get down to a good working relationship and not because he wanted to seduce me. Maybe I was flattering myself. Anyway, it all started badly, with him arriving on the stage fifteen minutes late, looking like he was ready to chew me into little pieces.

'We started to rehearse, and I found his method was rather improvisory, especially in the musical numbers which, of course, he could do almost without rehearsal while I was trying to figure out which was my left foot and which was my right. I was also rather overwhelmed at the thought that I was singing with Frank Sinatra! It went downhill from there.'

Shelley said that whenever his two children, Nancy and Frank Jr, came to the commissary, she would join them. 'Sometimes a priest from the Catholic Family Counselling Service would be with them, and whenever that priest, who was a very nice man, would spend time with Frank, he just became impossible during filming. Whatever the priest said to him always disturbed him so much that he just didn't seem to hear what anyone, including the director [Joseph Pevney], was saying to him.'

Because of all his troubles, Sinatra was losing weight drastically. Shelley said, 'He must have lost a pound every week, which made me look heavier as the film went on.'

The two stars had many arguments, which grew worse when they began night shooting at Burbank Airport. The scene called for them to have an argument, but the row grew into a real verbal slanging match. 'I can't remember what started the row,' said Shelley, 'but to give you an idea of how bad it got, the nicest things we called each other were "skinny, no-talent Hoboken bastard!" and "bow-legged bitch from Brooklyn!"'

Their arguments were highlighted by language so foul that the public who came to watch the shooting quickly disappeared, while Pevney tried to ease the situation by joking that he had made a mistake by not photographing their real argument.

By 3 a.m., with tiredness setting in and arguments still punctuating the shooting, Shelley finally slugged Sinatra. 'He had a bodyguard who was probably carrying a gun,' she recalled, 'and I was convinced he was going to shoot me then and there. Either that or I thought Frank would slug me back. But he didn't. He just got into his car and sped away. I guess I was lucky.'

Shelley went back to her apartment and called Western Union to send an angry telegram to Sinatra, which ran to three pages. Copies were sent to Sinatra's agent, Shelley's agent and the Universal directors in New York. In the morning, Shelley got a call from her agent, saying that the Universal brass wanted to meet with her and Sinatra at nine. Shelley refused to attend if Sinatra was to be there. She said she would only ever be in his presence when she actually had to act with him, and she wasn't sure she even wanted to do that any more.

The most important men from Universal were waiting for her when the agent took her to the meeting. Leo Spitz, the studio's finance boss, told Shelley, 'From all the rumour we hear, you're going to be nominated for a Best Actress Oscar for *A Place in the Sun*, so we need to keep your publicity as dignified as possible and maybe there's a good chance you'll win the Academy Award. We need to keep your fights with Mr Sinatra out of the press, and since most of the newspapers owe us favours, we can probably keep most if not all of it out of the papers. So you've got to calm down.'

He also went on to explain that Sinatra was going through 'a terrible and troubled period of his life and career'. He explained that Frank had periods when he actually lost his voice, which was terrifying him. 'You speak of humanity in that document you sent me,' he told Shelley. 'Perhaps you could examine your own humanity. And realise the terrible trouble that young man is in.' He told Shelly that she was at the top of her career and he asked her to try to understand the reasons why Sinatra was behaving so badly.

Shelley was told to be ready to shoot the final scene at 12.30 – a couple of other scenes had been cut from the script to bring filming to a speedy end. She was there on time, and climbed into bed on set to learn the newly written lines. Sinatra was there on time too: he had also been given a lecture by the Universal bosses, and Shelley expected everything to run smoothly. It did – through rehearsal. His final line was, 'I'll have a cup of coffee and leave you two lovebirds alone.'

Then they came to shoot it. The final line arrived, but this time Sinatra said, 'I'll have a cup of Jack Daniel's, or I'm gonna pull that blonde broad's hair by its black roots.'

Shelley reached for a prop bedpan and threw it at Sinatra.

Another row, even worse than the previous night's, erupted. The picture shut down as Shelley and Frank just refused to speak or work with each other. Universal had a picture with no ending.

Two days later, Shelley, who had shut her phone off, received a message from Nancy Sinatra, asking her to call her. Shelley did. Nancy was in tears as she explained, 'Frank can't get his 25,000 dollars if the picture isn't finished, and the bank has threatened to foreclose the mortgage on the house. My children will be out on the street. So please, Shelley, finish the picture.'

Shelley called the studio and said she'd return to work and that Sinatra 'could say any damn line he wanted to'. They did the scene, and Sinatra delivered the final line as written. The two stars went their separate ways.

Sinatra went to work on a weekly CBS television show, and Shelley was dismayed when she discovered that at the end of each show, he looked into the camera and, 'as if he were cursing', said, 'I leave you with two words . . . SHELLEY WINTERS.'

Shelley's lawyer, Jerry Giesler, wrote to CBS and to Sinatra's lawyer telling him to 'cease and desist', or be sued for millions. Finally, after several weeks of threats, Sinatra did cease, 'but it was probably because he didn't want to give me all that free publicity,' said Shelley.

Chapter Four

Sam the Cigar

Ava told me that it was impossible to be with Frank and not know he was 'in bed with the Mob'. She couldn't recall when she first became aware of this fact, but she claimed she had no idea he had such associations before she got involved with him. 'Otherwise,' she said, 'I think I would have avoided him like the plague.'

It was always a curious thing to hear Ava talk about Sinatra, because there was invariably a sparkle in her eye, and it was obvious that she never really fell out of love with him. She just fell out of love with his Mob lifestyle. Their many tempestuous arguments became a legend in Hollywood folklore and, more often than not, were put down to the fact that Sinatra was sleeping with other women, or to the fact that he was jealous over Ava's friendships (which she admitted were often more than mere friendships) with other men. What really destroyed their love, however, was his refusal to break his links with organised crime lords. Many years later he would prove to her that he was breaking away from his associations, but by then it was too late to mend fences and rebuild bridges. Nonetheless, my observation, and that of others, was that they never wholly fell out of love with each other.

There was nothing new about Hollywood folk mixing with the

underworld. Everyone in the business at that time knew it. It is difficult to understand how, then, with Frank Sinatra so caught up in it, and rumours abounding about his associations with gangsters, Ava should have been so ignorant of the fact when she started her affair with him. I sometimes wonder if, in her heart, she did know, or at least had heard all the rumours, but was so beguiled by him in the beginning that she was able to blank it from her mind, and so come to believe her claim that she never knew – until it was too late.

Ava recalled a day when Sam Giancana came to their home. Since taking over the Mob's activities in Hollywood, Mooney had made a point of getting to know those entertainers who were most susceptible to Mob influence. Frank Sinatra was one of them, and had probably known Giancana since 1947, possibly earlier. Ava said this occasion was the first time she had met Giancana. 'What a weasel,' she said. 'He liked to think he had charm, but I couldn't see it.'

She had heard Frank talk about Sam the Cigar and she was not at all happy to meet him. She told me, 'I mean, this guy had had people killed – and had killed people himself. What's to like about a cold-blooded killer? But Francis welcomed him like a brother. I once asked him, "Why the hell do you mix with these gangsters?"

'He said, "I don't remember a time in my life when I didn't have friends like these. They were my parents' friends. They got me started in the business. You don't understand. These guys are just businessmen. With me, it's just business. You can't work in the clubs and not do business with them."

'I said, "Yeah, but you seem to *love* doing business with them."

'He said, "My business is none of your business." And I could feel a fight coming on, so I shut up.'

Giancana had indeed come to talk business. He knew Sinatra's career was in trouble, and he came offering him work in the Mob-run clubs. Ava said that she realised he could have turned down Giancana's offer of work, but that might well have been a big mistake. Sinatra's downhill spiral seemed out of control and he, and she, knew it might end in one of only two ways – either total career meltdown, or a chance to work and maybe get back on top.

The thing Ava came to realise was that Giancana wasn't about to give Sinatra a helping hand unless, at some point, Sinatra would be big enough to make Giancana huge profits. Sam the Cigar knew his business, and he didn't invest in failure. Giancana would see to it that Sinatra would get back on top, and that would prove fruitful for both Frank and Sam.

As far as Sinatra was concerned, failure wasn't an option, and so he was glad to accept Giancana's offer. Ava remembered Giancana telling him, 'Frank, you're going to be a fucking hit again, and when you are, we're both going to make so much fucking dough, we'll be fucking kings.'

'Sam Giancana just couldn't finish a sentence without fucking swearing,' said Ava.

It was around that time that Sinatra heard he might be called before the Kefauver hearings. Ava recalled that he was terrified at the prospect of being exposed on television for having connections with the Mafia. She told him, 'You've only got yourself to blame for going over to Cuba.' She admitted she did not show much sympathy towards him, but she was afraid of what such exposure would do to him.

Through Sinatra's attorney, Sol Gelb, a secret meeting was arranged between Frank and Joseph Nellis on the top floor of the Rockefeller Center. Nellis produced a selection of photographs, one of them showing Sinatra standing on the balcony of the Hotel Nacional with an arm around Luciano. Another was of him getting off the plane at Havana with the attaché case, in the company of the Fischettis.

Given the existence of these photographs, Sinatra was unable to deny his presence in Cuba or his meeting with Lucky Luciano. When Nellis suggested that the attaché case had been full of money – as much as one million dollars – Sinatra claimed the case was packed with personal items.

Nellis tried another line of attack, asking Sinatra if he was aware what line of business Luciano was in. Sinatra maintained that he wasn't. Nellis asked about his associations with men like Bugsy Siegel, Meyer Lansky and Frank Costello. Sinatra he said he knew them only to say 'hello' and 'goodbye' to.

Then Sinatra, his stress turning into anger, accused Nellis of wanting to put him in front of the television cameras just because he happened to have met the people he was investigating, and so ruin his career. Nellis told him, 'Nobody wants to ruin you, Mr Sinatra.'

He asked Frank if he knew Willie Moretti. Sinatra said that Moretti had arranged some dates for him to perform when he first got started, insisting, 'I have never had any business dealings with any of those men.'

After two hours in which Sinatra sweated pints, Nellis was left with the conclusion that Sinatra would be of no help at the hearings, and he escaped what would certainly have been an untimely end to his career.

The Kefauver hearings might well have broken the back of organised crime once and for all, had it not been for the intervention of Senator Joseph McCarthy, who decided that Communism was the greatest danger America faced, and the public focus quickly shifted from the Mafia to the Communists. Nobody cared any longer about the gangsters who had been exposed on television. In the Mafia itself, however, it was realised that the old-order mobsters could no longer function efficiently. Bosses began dying off at an alarming rate.

The first to be killed, in October 1951, was Frank Sinatra's long-time friend Willie Moretti, who was lured into a restaurant and held back in a chair while bullets were pumped into him.

Frank Costello was luckier: he spent the next five years in and out of prison for tax evasion charges, as well as for walking out on the congressional committee.

Sam Giancana was still only an underboss of Chicago, although, through Johnny Roselli, he ruled Hollywood. Giancana actually detested entertainers. He said that everyone in Hollywood was 'waiting to be used'. Movie stars, he said, were 'worthless bums and whores'.

Once Sinatra felt safe from being called to testify by Senator Kefauver, he openly dated Ava and attended the premiere of her latest film, *Show Boat*, in July 1951. There followed a brief holiday in Mexico, after which Frank announced that he and Ava were officially engaged.

Ava's and Frank's tempestuous affair continued in the usual way – passionate lovemaking and furious arguments. After one such row, Sinatra took an overdose of sleeping tablets, which turned out not to be fatal, but it was another of his attempts to get her attention. Ava told me, 'All I really wanted to do was punch the sorry bastard for doing that to me, but on the other hand, I also realised just how desperate he was for me – and so his stupid game worked, because I just fell more in love with him.'

Further pressure was put upon their relationship when Nancy decided to contest the divorce. It was also plain that, while Frank's career was in decline, Ava's was reaching its peak, and that was a real blow to his ego. The pressure took its toll on Ava, and she collapsed in the autumn of 1951 and spent weeks in hospital. Without her, Frank just seemed to go downhill ever faster, physically and professionally. He told friends he was tired of living – something they had become used to with his vague attempts at suicide – but this time he really meant it. He went home and turned on the gas stove, and would have died if a friend hadn't found him.

Ava never knew anything about it. It was a hushed-up episode, the one time he didn't want her to know what he'd tried to do. Frank's and Nancy's divorce was granted in October 1951, and he married Ava on 7 November. Life seemed to be getting better at last.

Yet the marriage was doomed before it started. As Ava told me, 'When it was good, it was very good, but when things got bad, it was like a fucking war zone.'

The trouble with Frank was that, as mad as he was about Ava, surely one of the most beautiful and alluring women in Hollywood history – and a wild cat in bed – he couldn't resist other women. Ava told me, 'People ask me which role was my biggest challenge. My role as Frank's wife was the biggest challenge of my life.' What really destroyed the marriage, however, was Frank's relationship with the likes of Sam Giancana. 'In the beginning Francis thought of Giancana as a brother,' she told me. 'I sometimes thought that he loved him more than he loved me.'

In May 1951, Giancana's popularity among the Italian community grew when he was one of the main sponsors for an annual charitable event, 'Night of Stars', on behalf of the Italian Welfare Council. It was actually a very good and legitimate cause, with all the proceeds going straight to poor children. However, Sam the Cigar sent his own men to visit businesses and wealthy individuals to persuade them to attend the event at extravagant prices.

Giancana personally enlisted entertainers such as Frank Sinatra, Dean Martin, Jerry Lewis, Jimmy Durante and Bob Hope. His 'influence' over entertainers was just one of his great powers that threatened to topple the men who ran the Chicago Mafia, Tony Accardo and Paul Ricca. He also had Johnny Roselli dealing with the CIA. Roselli had secured the co-operation of the billionaire Howard Hughes, who, Roselli told Giancana, had 'Vice President Nixon eating out of his hand'. Hughes, said

Roselli, had 'Washington paid off'. Giancana was gradually taking over America, with Roselli making deals with the CIA, while Howard Hughes worked with the old-time mobster Murray Humphreys to maintain a hold over J Edgar Hoover.

Meanwhile, Frank was having a crisis in his career. He was dropped by CBS, by his agents MCA and by Columbia Records, and he begged his Mob friends to find him work in their own nightclubs. To help him out, the Palladinos – Joseph 'Beans' Palladino and Joseph 'Little Beans' Jr – engaged him at the Copa in Boston. Vincent Teresa, a mobster who revealed all in a book called *My Life in the Mafia*, wrote, 'He did all right, not sensational, but all right. Then he went to Joe Beans and asked if he could borrow money.' Frank said he'd pay back the money straight out of his fee from his next performance at the Copa, which he did do in 1953, at the time when his comeback movie, *From Here to Eternity*, was about to be released.

Speculation continues over whether the Mafia had any influence on Sinatra's getting the role of Maggio in *From Here to Eternity*, which brought him a Best Supporting Actor Oscar. It was the episode from Mario Puzo's *The Godfather* in which a businessman wakes up to find the head of his dead horse in bed with him that gave rise to the myth that this was what happened to the Columbia boss Harry Cohn by way of persuading him to cast Sinatra.

Ava Gardner told me that Harry Cohn didn't even own a horse. She also said that Harry Cohn, like all the major studio heads of the day, did have links – often without choice – to the Mob. It just so happened that Cohn had stronger links than most movie moguls did, and she was well aware that he appeased the Mob on numerous occasions by helping the artists the Mafia were sponsoring.

Although it was always denied – with or without the horse-head incident – that Cohn was persuaded to give Sinatra the part by the Mafia, Ava suspected it was true. This was at a time when

Sam Giancana had promised Frank help in getting back on top, and although Ava never knew the details, she said, 'Of course Francis got the part because of those fucking hoods he called his friends.'

Regardless of how the Mob were coercing Cohn, however, the film's director Fred Zinnemann insisted to me, 'If I hadn't wanted Frank Sinatra, I wouldn't have cast him.' Sinatra was so desperate to do the film that he accepted a meagre flat fee of eight thousand dollars.

The big stars of the film were Burt Lancaster, Montgomery Clift and Deborah Kerr. Sinatra was just a supporting actor. Burt Lancaster told me, 'In the beginning we had a lotta fun. Every night we'd all go to dinner together – Fred Zinnemann, Deborah, Frank and Monty. One night Frank was going mad trying to get through to Ava on the phone – she was in Africa filming [*Mogambo*] with Clark Gable, and we'd all just kid him about being jealous of Gable. The thing was, Frank was *really* jealous. I knew Ava well and I guess he had reason not to trust her too much.

'We continued having fun until Harry Cohn insisted that the big drunk scene with Monty and Frank be played standing up instead of sitting down as it was written. Cohn and Zinnemann had a big argument over that, but even Zinnemann had to give in, and when he told Frank and Monty they had to do the scene standing, Frank got into an argument with Zinnemann, and after that they never spoke to each other socially again. That brought all the fun to a stop.'

James Jones, who wrote the book on which the screenplay was based, spent a great deal of time in Hawaii, where the film was being shot. 'He hung out with Monty and Frank all the time,' said Lancaster, 'and they'd get drunk, and always Frank would go on about Ava. He talked to me a lot about Ava – he was just obsessed with her.'

Jones, Clift and Sinatra became a trio who got drunk together every night, especially when they returned to Hollywood to film the interiors. With Ava still in Africa, Sinatra became so depressed that he told Clift he was going to kill himself. Clift talked him out of it.

They would often return at night to the Roosevelt Hotel, where they were all staying, and become loud and obnoxious, throwing beer cans out of the window at passers-by. Twice the hotel manager threatened to throw them out, and both times Columbia had to intervene. Harry Cohn began to regret giving Sinatra a break.

After filming was complete, Clift and Sinatra remained close friends. By this time Sinatra must have known, as did everyone else, that Clift was a homosexual. He never showed any contempt or prejudice, however: Sinatra had always disliked prejudice of any kind. Then, one night at a party in Bel Air, Sinatra saw Clift make advances to another man – and Frank had his bodyguards throw Clift out. That was the end of the friendship.

From Here to Eternity was not only a huge success, but it went on to win seven Academy Awards, including one for Sinatra as Best Supporting Actor. He was back on top.

Giancana was delighted for Sinatra, but the Palladinos became unhappy with him. They asked him to come back to the Copa and so bring in the crowds, but he never accepted their offer – and for that, the Boston Mob never forgave him. He was lucky to have Sam Giancana as his friend. Without Sam's patronage, Sinatra might well have paid the full price for thumbing his nose at the powerful Palladinos.

Giancana was finding Sinatra work, although after *From Here to Eternity* Frank didn't really need his help any more. Yet he couldn't resist the offers Giancana threw his way. In fact, said Ava, it really came down to Frank doing Giancana favours by agreeing to sing in his clubs. When Ava told him, 'You don't need that asshole any more,' he replied, 'I know I don't, but I owe him. I don't welch on a friend.'

Ava argued that Giancana would one day prove he was no friend, and that simply started another furious row. Many of their arguments, Ava said, were about his Mob friends. 'I could maybe have coped with him fucking other women,' she said, 'but I couldn't put up with him fucking – or getting fucked by – the Mob.'

Chapter Five

A Mob Lifestyle

Although Ava loved Frank's wild side, she hated the fact that he took it to extremes. He was, she said, learning how to be a hood, and it showed in his behaviour and attitude, especially during the late fifties and into the sixties. 'I swear he would, at that time, have preferred to be a don than an entertainer,' she once remarked. 'He became, for a while, a dangerous man to cross. Thank God he finally learned his lesson – although you still wouldn't want to cross him in anything.'

Being a spirited woman, Ava didn't bother trying to be nice whenever she encountered Giancana. She would either avoid making eye contact – and certainly never spoke to him unless she really had to – or just glare at him. One day, with Sinatra out of earshot, he asked her why she hated him.

She said, 'What makes you think I hate you?'

'Because you show no fucking respect,' he replied.

'What makes you think you deserve my respect?'

'Because I'm your husband's friend. He shows me respect.'

'That's because Francis is a bad judge of character.'

Ava remembered how Giancana became flushed with anger. She was sure that, if she hadn't been Frank's wife, he would have hit her. She just glared at him without blinking, and even jutted her beautiful dimpled chin, just daring him to strike. She knew she was shaming him, and to hide the fact he burst into laughter and said nothing more to her.

She also recounted a day when she and Frank ran into Johnny Roselli. 'What a sleaze he was,' she said. He had come to ask a favour of Sinatra. There was a young starlet – Ava wouldn't name her as she eventually became a famous movie star – who needed a helping hand, and Roselli wanted Sinatra to give it.

Sinatra, who despised Roselli, said, 'I'll help anyone if I like them and feel they deserve it. But I won't do it just because you ask me to.'

'You don't seem to get the point,' said Roselli. 'I'm not asking you. I'm telling you.'

Frank squared up to Roselli and told him, 'You don't tell me anything. You can ask, but don't ever tell me.'

'You wanna tell Sam that?'

'Sam don't treat me like a bellhop. He asks me a favour, I'll do what I can. *You* ask me, and you say *please*. But don't you ever *tell* me. You got it?'

Roselli was just as arrogant as Sinatra was, and Ava feared the argument would come to blows – or even worse. So she stepped in and said, 'Francis, why not meet the girl and see what you think?'

Sinatra didn't like Ava interfering and turned on her, almost unable to help himself, saying, 'You keep your beautiful nose out of our business.'

There were several moments of disquieting silence between the two men. Finally Roselli smiled and said, 'All I'm *asking* is that you meet with her.'

Frank agreed. All Ava would say further on that episode was that Sinatra met the young woman and, feeling she had definite potential, had a word in the right ear, and the starlet was on her way to stardom. He made every effort to keep Roselli out of the situation, but the actress concerned found herself inextricably in debt to the Mob. After that, Frank made sure that when he gave anyone any help in their career, it was on his terms and not the Mob's.

There was, said Ava, a truly generous side to Frank's nature. The only problem was that anyone he helped generally found themselves in debt to *him*. That, she said, was simply his way – because it was the Mafia's way. Fortunately, the worst thing that could happen to someone who owed Sinatra and then did something to offend him was to find that he would refuse to speak to them ever again. The Mafia had more drastic ways of dealing with those who crossed them.

A few days after the heated exchange between Sinatra and Roselli, something happened that, Ava said, 'scared the crap out of me'. Roselli had taken great exception to the way Sinatra had refused to just do as he was told. One night Frank and Ava returned to their Los Angeles home and had hardly got inside the door when three men turned up and barged in. Ava was pushed to the floor by one while the other two grabbed Sinatra and held him back.

'What the fuck is this?' screamed Sinatra.

The one who had pushed Ava to the floor told him, 'We're going to teach you a lesson.'

Sinatra did not know these three men, but he realised immediately that they were Mob guys who had been called in from various states. That was the Mafia's way, to bring in hit men from out of state. Ava was convinced they were both about to be murdered.

'Who sent you?' asked Sinatra. 'Was it Roselli?'

He didn't get an answer. The two who held him pushed him into a chair. Ava tried to get up, but was told, 'You stay where you are.'

'You hurt her and I'll fucking kill the lot of you,' yelled Sinatra.

The three men just laughed at him. 'All by yourself?' one of them asked.

'Let me out of this chair and we'll see who's the last man standing.'

Ava knew he didn't stand a chance, but she was ready to join in if Frank did manage to get to his feet and start throwing fists.

The three men towered over him, and he was sure he was either in for a beating or an untimely death. 'You can't kill me,' he told them. 'Sam the Cigar will have your fucking heads.'

Again they laughed, and that suggested to Sinatra that Giancana might well be behind all this. He prepared himself for whatever came, but they didn't lay into him as he expected. Instead, they began smashing up the place, turning over furniture, breaking a mirror, smashing picture frames, tearing out the telephone wire, and generally wrecking the entire room. One of them was about to demolish Sinatra's bar, but one of the others said, 'Leave that alone. We could all do with a drink.'

While Frank stayed in his chair and Ava remained on the floor, the three men helped themselves to Frank's stock of brandy, Scotch and Jack Daniel's – his favourite beverage. Ava said it was their way of taunting Frank, who just sat still and glared at them with what she described as 'eyes that had killer burned into them'. She was absolutely positive that, had Frank decided to take action, he would have made a very real attempt to kill them and would probably have got himself, and her, killed in the process. She kept looking at him, trying to catch his eye, mouthing the word 'No' and making a little shake of the head.

One of the men took hold of a fallen chair, put it upright and sat down right in front of Frank. 'Now it's like this,' he said. 'The next time you get asked to do something, you fucking do it. Got it?'

'I don't know what you're talking about.'

One of the other men moved as if to strike Sinatra in the mouth. The sitting man said, 'No! We don't touch him. Mr Sinatra needs his mouth in good shape. Ain't that right, Mr Sinatra? He's gotta be able to sing, or Mooney won't like it.'

'So Sam sent you,' said Sinatra.

'Sam who?'

Ava thought to herself that Frank was about to talk himself into a beating whether Giancana wanted it or not.

The sitting man said, 'Don't ask questions, and you won't get your fucking head broken.'

Frank leaned forward defiantly. 'Let me tell you something. Sam is my friend, and he knows I'll do anything for him.'

'No one's talking about Sam.'

'Then it's gotta be that fucking Roselli.'

'Paint the picture for yourself, Mr Sinatra. I'm sure you know what this is all about.'

'I'm beginning to get the picture.'

'That's all you have to do.'

With that, the three men finished their drinks and left.

Frank rushed over to Ava to help her up, but she shook him off. She was furious with him. 'Look what you've fucking done! You get yourself tied in with the fucking Mob and all this shit happens.'

He said, 'Calm down. Let me get you a drink.'

'I don't want a fucking drink!' she yelled – and then poured herself a drink. 'I want you to finish with these bastards before they kill us.'

'No one's gonna kill us. I'm gonna talk to Sam about this. This is Roselli's work.'

'You know fucking well that Roselli doesn't do this sort of thing unless Giancana tells him to.'

That made Sinatra reconsider, but he still picked up the phone, saying, 'I'll call Sam now and sort this out.' Then he remembered that the phone line had been ripped out.

Ava recalled that the rest of their argument was as furious as any row they'd ever had, with Ava telling Frank he'd brought all this on them, and Frank telling her he'd only ever done what he thought would be good for his career and their lives together.

There was no question of their calling the police. The next day they had all the broken furnishings discreetly removed and new ones brought in. When the phone line was repaired, Sinatra called Giancana in Chicago and told him what had happened.

Sam denied all knowledge of it, and claimed he was furious with Roselli for calling in the three men to break up Frank's home. He said he'd tell Roselli in no uncertain terms that he should never take action without checking it with him first.

That seemed to satisfy Sinatra, but Ava told him – and told me – that she couldn't believe that Johnny Roselli would have acted without Giancana's orders. That caused another row. Their 'domestic arguments' were, said Ava, enough to wreck any marriage, but their arguments about Frank's involvement with Giancana and other Mafia bosses were what really killed it.

There was another incident that Ava recalled. Frank had been engaged to perform at one of the many clubs the Mafia ran. There was Sinatra, on the stage, singing to a packed crowd, while alone at a table at the front sat Ava. She liked it that way. She just wanted to sit, smoke and drink, and watch and listen to 'the best singer in the world'. During the romantic songs, Frank would look at Ava and smile, and, knowing that he was privately dedicating the song to her, she would smile back. When Ava smiled, she was just simply sexy, and Frank loved that. If he could get her to smile, it got his hormones racing.

Unfortunately, the smile on Ava's face disappeared when two men joined her. She didn't know who they were, but they had recognised her and, as it turned out, they had been told by Sinatra that there would be room for them at her table. He had not, however, mentioned to Ava that she would be joined by two strangers.

She said she knew immediately that these were Mob guys. She refused to look at them, even though they made some polite comments about how lovely she looked and told her, 'That husband of yours knows how to sing.' They even introduced themselves, but she ignored them and never did remember their names. She sat with her arms folded, her legs crossed, her face as cold as stone. Frank, on stage, continued to perform, but he saw that Ava was not best pleased, and it threw his concentration.

He reached the point where he told the audience, 'I'm just going to take a little break now,' and he came down from the stage and sat at the table with Ava and her unwelcome guests. The hoods congratulated him and said how pleased they were that the place was filled because of him. He introduced Ava to them – although she ignored the introductions – and then said to them, 'Will you excuse me while Ava and I have a dance?' Ava recalled that they were still extremely polite, and had it not been for the fact that she 'could smell a fucking hood a mile away', she would have thought them just a couple of well-dressed gentlemen.

On the small dance floor, Frank and Ava moved in unison, but he could see that her mind was not on the dance movements. He said, 'I know you're mad at me.'

She said nothing.

'These guys run the place,' he continued. 'What else can I do when my employers tell me they want to meet you and watch the show with you?'

She replied coldly, 'You could have talked it over with me first.'

'I know I should have. But I know what you would have said.'

'So you were too fucking scared to tell me.'

He admitted he was, and he became so apologetic, to the point of being pathetic, that for once she decided not to turn what should be a lovely romantic moment into another tempestuous fight. She told me, 'I could see he had no choice, and I was tired of giving him the same argument about how he shouldn't have got involved with those hoods in the first place. But they were giving him work, and I knew – even though I didn't like it – that if he was going to work, he was going to be like every other entertainer of that time and have gangsters for employers.'

'Let's just hold each other close and forget about them for a few moments,' he told her. She nodded, and held him tighter.

'When the dance is over, I'd really like to leave,' she said softly.

He understood, and said that he would arrange for a car to drive her to their hotel.

When Frank returned alone to the table, the two men asked where Ava was. He told them, 'She hasn't been feeling well all day, so she's calling it an early night.'

One of them said, 'Yeah, she looked kinda sour when we sat down. Poor girl. Hope she feels better soon.'

Then Frank got back up on stage and continued to sing. What he didn't know was that Ava had gone back to the hotel having virtually made up her mind that it was never going to work between them. And that, she said, was a shame because she was so in love with him.

But no matter how much she loved him, it was not enough for him to break his links to the Mob, and in 1953 he was engaged to sing at the Sands Hotel in Las Vegas, which was run by Joseph 'Doc' Statcher, one of the New Jersey mob. Statcher, unlike the Palladinos, was fond of Sinatra and allowed him to buy a two-per-cent share of the Sands for 54,000 dollars. Another two per cent went to George Raft.

By the end of 1953 Ava and Frank had separated, and she had gone off to Spain to have an affair with another bullfighter. She filed for divorce in 1954. Frank began an affair with another actress, one with whom he would fall in love – even while he was still in love with Ava – and who would be the catalyst for what would become his own personal vendetta against one of the most powerful Mafia bosses of all time. That actress was Marilyn Monroe.

*

In 1953 Sinatra made *Young at Heart* with Doris Day. One of his
co-stars was Gig Young. In 1970 I spent some time with Young,
who treated me to a show at the famous Raymond's Revue Bar,
Soho's most exclusive strip joint. He told me that, had this been
Las Vegas, the place would have been run by the Mafia. He then
went into a story about working with Frank Sinatra and how
Frank introduced him to Johnny Roselli.

Gig and Frank had something in common: they both liked to
drink. After work, they occasionally got together to down a few
Scotches and some Jack Daniel's at a small restaurant in
Hollywood which Frank particularly liked. Into the place one day
came Johnny Roselli.

Young recalled, 'As soon as Frank saw Roselli, his eyes went
cold. But as Roselli approached us, he put on a smile and said,
"Johnny, join us." So Roselli sat down.'

Young had heard of Johnny Roselli, but said he 'had not had
the displeasure of meeting him before'. Sinatra and Roselli, he
said, put on a 'great show' of being close friends, but he had the
distinct impression that Frank really didn't like him at all – which
surprised Young, as he knew very well that Frank had friends in
the Mob.

Roselli said to Young, 'I know you. You're quite an actor.
Mainly in B pictures, though.'

Although Young knew he was right, he defended himself by
saying that he had been nominated for an Academy Award for
Come Fill the Cup in 1951.

'Yeah, but you were only a supporting actor in that. Once
you've been nominated as Best Supporting Actor, you stay a
supporting actor. Now, what you really want is to be a top star,
like Frankie here.'

Young replied that it didn't bother him being a supporting
player, just so long as he kept on working.

Roselli seemed adamant that he wanted to do Gig a big favour by putting in a good word for him at various studios and getting him elevated to leading man.

Young politely declined his offer. 'I'm happy being a working actor.'

Roselli did not give up. He kept on about how Gig ought to let him handle things and see to it that he got bigger parts 'like we did for Frankie'.

All this time, Sinatra had kept quiet, but he was gradually getting wound up and when Roselli made mention of the help his associates had given to him, Frank said, 'Look, Johnny, Gig said he don't want no help, so leave him alone.'

That caused Roselli to pause a moment, and then he said, 'Frankie, I don't know what's eating you, but you know better than most that I could really help Gig.'

Frank said very firmly, 'Gig don't want your help.'

Roselli replied, 'Let's let Gig decide.'

'I already told you,' said Young, still maintaining a polite demeanour. He told me he didn't dare speak to Roselli the way Frank did, as he was sure he'd pay the price if he did.

Roselli then went on at length about how much he could really do for Gig, if only he'd give him the chance. Every time Young told him he didn't want his help, 'but thanks very much', Roselli did his best to persuade Young that he was kidding himself if he didn't want to be a major star 'like Frankie'.

Sinatra said, 'You keep mentioning my name, Johnny, and I'd like you to stop.'

'What's the matter, Frankie? You unhappy being on top again?'

Gig said that Sinatra just glared at him, saying nothing. After a 'long, pregnant pause during which I was convinced fists would start flying', Young broke in with, 'Tell you what, Johnny, I'll think it over and get back to you.'

Roselli replied, 'Make sure you do,' as though it wasn't an option. Then he got up and left.

'Jesus, Gig, what did you tell him that for?' asked Sinatra.

'I thought discretion was the better part of valour at a time like this. The guy wasn't going to give up.'

'And he won't, believe me. But don't worry. I'll make sure he leaves you alone.'

Then Sinatra gave Young a discourse on the virtues of being a supporting actor and how such a career would probably last longer than that of any top star. 'When you're at the top, there's only one way to go eventually – down. Believe me, I've been there.'

'Yeah, Frank, but you climbed back up again.'

'Like the man said, I had help. Look, Gig, I like doing it the way I do it, but it ain't right for everyone, and I don't think it's right for you.'

'You mean, you don't think I've got what it takes to be a major star?'

'That's not what I'm saying at all. So don't take offence. Look, I know the way Roselli does business, and I'm doing you a big favour by telling you it ain't right for you. At least, not his way. If you want to make it to the top, do it your own way.'

Young just smiled and lifted his glass to toast Sinatra, saying, 'Here's to you, Frank, because you're one of the few honest guys who ever gave me advice and told me the way it is.'

Sinatra relaxed then, enjoying the compliment, and raised his glass also. Thereafter he and Young got on well, and Gig was forever grateful that he had Frank Sinatra with him the day the Mafia tried to make him an offer he was wise to refuse.

By 1955 Sinatra's film career was gaining momentum. He had the talent to be able to alternate between musicals and straight drama – but he just couldn't stop himself from using Mob-style tactics to get his own way. He had gained a reputation for being a tough guy, an image that did not impress everyone with whom he worked. One such man was Lee Marvin, who co-starred with Sinatra in *Not as a Stranger* in 1955. Lee, a man who could punch with the best of them, told me in 1984:

'I had always admired Sinatra as a singer, and I envied him his role in *From Here to Eternity*. But as a man, I was less charmed. I remember one day he was getting shitty about something to do with what I was doing, and I told him I didn't take shit from anyone. And I didn't. I mean, I got into fights over the drop of a hat. I was a mean bastard when I wanted to be – still am. But in those days I liked to booze and carouse my way through life, although I took my work seriously – most of the time.

'So there was little Frankie Sinatra squaring up to me: he must have got a crick in his neck looking up at me 'cos I towered over him. I guess, thinking back, I have to admire his guts. But on the other hand, he was just pushing his weight around, all because he had gangsters for friends. We all knew it. He would boast, "I can get your legs broken with a snap of my fingers," which is what he told me that day.

'So I told him, "I was a marine while you were dodging the draft, and I could snap your neck with one twist."

'He didn't like that. He said, "You wanna take me on here and now?"

'I said, "Any time you like."

'He would've laid into me too, if it hadn't been for [Robert] Mitchum who waded in and got between us. Sinatra told him, "Get the fuck out of my way. I'm gonna kill the punk."

'So Bob told him, "You couldn't kill him if he had both his hands tied behind his back."

'And Sinatra said, "I'll take you on, too."

'"No you won't," said Bob, "because if you do, you'll be the one who winds up dead and then we'll have to reshoot all your scenes, and that would really piss me off."

'Now Sinatra was really like, you don't seem to know who I

am, and we knew all right. Bob just said, "Wait till we finish the picture, and then you can take us both on."

'He said, "Right."

'For a few days Bob and I wondered if we'd end up with cement shoes or something, because we knew he had his Mob friends and we'd shamed him, which you just don't do to any hood – and that's what Sinatra thought he was in those days. I'm happy to say he's changed his tune.

'Anyway, a few days passed, and things were kinda tense between us, and then he apologised, saying he'd had some personal matter that had upset him and he shouldn't have been taking it out on me. We shook hands, and everything was just fine after that. So you could say he did the right thing, which showed he was bigger than he stood – and I didn't get thrown into the river wearing concrete shoes.'

Lee did come to like Sinatra in later years, but, for a long time, they didn't talk.

The film's director, Stanley Kramer, also had his reasons for disliking Sinatra. He said:

'The guy was a hoodlum. Not in the worst sense, but bad enough. He had his Mafia friends, and I'd heard that they'd put a metaphoric gun to Harry Cohn's head to get him the part of Maggio in *From Here to Eternity*, but no one put any kind of a gun to my head. But that's how it felt so often with Sinatra. Right on the first day, it was, "You're dealing with me now, not some pansy out of stage school."

'So I'm saying, "What do you mean, Frank?"

'"I mean you can't push me around!"

'I'm guessing he must have been having a bad time with Ava or some woman, but that's still no way to talk to me. I said, "Who's pushing you around, Frank?"

'He just said, "I'm just letting you know, that's all."

'So I told him, "This isn't Chicago, Frank. You're not a

character out of a James Cagney movie."

'He said, "You're fucking lucky to have me in this picture."

'I think he meant that because he'd won an Oscar, he could call the shots, but even the biggest Oscar winner in the world doesn't expect to walk on the set and call the shots – well, some do. It's the director who calls the shots – on my pictures anyway – but with Sinatra, you get a guy who thinks he's the Hollywood Mafia. Even George Raft, who really was tied in with the Mob in a very real way, didn't act like that. He was a perfect gentleman, so I said to Sinatra, "Take a page out of Raft's book. Be nice to people. You might even like it."

'He suddenly starts backing off with his hands up, saying, "Don't get me wrong, Stanley. I'm nice to my friends. I like to find out who my friends are."

'I said, "What you mean is, you like to know who's gonna suck up to you and get all intimidated by this little tough-guy routine."

'He said, "Oh, believe me, it's no routine."

'I said, "I can believe it. But it won't work with me."

'He said, "Like I told you, I'm just letting you know."

'So I said, "Now let me let you know something. I see one guy around the set who I think even smells like a gangster, I'm shutting down the picture, I'm gonna recast you, and I'm gonna have the Screen Actors Guild ban you from ever making another picture in this country. You can go to fucking Sicily and make nice with the Mafia there."

'He said, "Don't ever use that word around me."

'I said, "What word – Mafia? Frank, everyone knows who your friends are, so don't give me any bullshit. I call it as I see it, and I see you for what you are."

'And so it went on, and finally we got on with the shooting, but he caused so much friction, I swore I'd never work with him again. Only I did so, because we couldn't get Marlon Brando to do *The Pride and the Passion* and by then Sinatra was so big, I let myself get talked into letting him do the part.'

Somewhere in the middle of all this turmoil on the set of *Not as a Stranger* was Robert Mitchum, who acted as peacemaker without making a big show of it. In 1977, he said:

'I think Frank's problem with Stanley was simply that this was the first film Stanley had ever directed. He'd produced a lot of films, but never directed before, and Frank was wary of him. The thing I discovered about Frank was that he liked to put on a show of being tough, partly for the sake of those he was working with, but also for those who, shall we say, sponsored him. He had a lot to live up to in those days as far as his Mafia cronies were concerned. I once said to him, "Frank, you're all curtain, aren't you?"

'He said, "What's that supposed to mean?"

'I said, "You hide behind this flashy curtain because you know you're a star, but pull the curtain back and behind it you're really a nice guy."

'He said, "I just don't like bad manners. If people are polite to me, I'm polite to them. Nobody should get away with not being polite to me."

'I said, "Yeah, Frank, but how about being polite to them first, and maybe you'll get some respect back?"

'He smiled and said, "Yeah, but I don't like to give 'em the edge over me. So I come in, guns blazing."

'That's how he dealt with the situation in those days, but he's mellowed now. In those days he had his Mob friends to impress. Today they ain't around, as far as I can see.

'Poor Stanley had to put up with a bunch of actors who loved to drink and loved a good fight – Lee Marvin, Broderick Crawford, me and Frank Sinatra. One day we had all had two or three drinks too many, and we had our own bar-room fight in a dressing room. We destroyed the place. Smashed up the furniture, threw the telephone, and poor Broderick ended up being thrown from a second-storey balcony. He didn't mind. It was just our way of having fun.

'I'll tell you something about Sinatra. Once you were on his wavelength, you had no trouble. He turned up for work one morning hung over and looking like a hound dog – which I always felt was my own exclusive expression, drunk or sober – so I laid him down on an operating table, which was part of the set, and placed pieces of cloth soaked in witch hazel over his eyes, and then I gave him a rub down with alcohol. That put him to sleep, and when he woke up, he saw me standing over him, and he muttered, "Mother!"

'Every year after that he sent me the most awfully sentimental Mother's Day cards. So you had to learn how to treat him, and then he was your friend. But, boy, was it hard work, just to get on the right side of him. In this business, you have to do that – make every effort to get on with your co-stars. I try to, but Frank: he just pushed you into either loving or hating him.'

While Frank Sinatra was using his Mob tactics to make friends and enemies in Hollywood in 1955, the tax men at the IRS were taking a great interest in the affairs of Tony Accardo and Paul Ricca, the bosses of Chicago. The two men decided to stand down from power, and Sam Giancana was duly elected the new boss of the Chicago Mob – only he would always prefer to call it the Outfit.

During the latter part of the fifties, Sam Giancana partied his way around Hollywood, Las Vegas, New York and Havana, mixing with top stars, especially those who were associated in some way with Frank Sinatra, such as Peter Lawford, Sammy Davis Jr and Natalie Wood. He loved the fact that hanging around Frank Sinatra were always groups of girls – or 'party girls', as he called them – all looking to either sleep with the stars or become a star. Giancana took full advantage of them.

Yet Sam the Cigar never overcame his contempt for entertainers, who, he said, were just 'prima donnas'. They were good for his business, however, because many of them were just unable to live within their income, and there was always someone asking Giancana for a cash loan. He charged a high interest rate. Out of respect for Sinatra, he treated the stars like his best friends – and few owed Giancana more than Frank Sinatra did.

Sam actually had a genuine fondness for Sinatra. To Giancana, Sinatra had class – which meant that not only was he a top entertainer, but he lived a lifestyle that reflected his associations with the Mob.

Chapter Six

Marilyn

Frank Sinatra and Marilyn Monroe had known each other for some years. While she was married to Joe DiMaggio, the couple would socialise with Frank and Ava. When their respective marriages broke up, they gave each other a certain amount of lustful solace.

When Marilyn announced, in January 1955, that she was setting up Marilyn Monroe Productions, she invited a party of friends to celebrate at the Copacabana, where Sinatra was taking the stage. The show was already sold out, but Marilyn, with Frank's help, had no trouble in getting an extra table prepared on the dance floor. When Frank saw her, he literally stopped the show, and smiled and winked at her as she sat down with her friends.

Frank had other reasons for knowing Marilyn, too. She was one of those chosen by Johnny Roselli and Sam Giancana to nurture into stardom.

Marilyn knew Roselli well, but it seems she had not met Giancana – although that would change just a week before her death. Giancana had always said, from the time he saw her famous nude photo on the *Playboy* calendar, that he wanted to bed her.

As Roselli and Sinatra were not the best of friends, Ava believed that Frank took it upon himself to try to protect her as much as he could without too much interference from his Mafia friends. Yet Roselli managed to win Monroe's trust – which would be her undoing in the end. Everyone in Hollywood knew he was no real agent, and he knew they knew, but he maintained his pose as a freelance agent. His association with Giancana made him a powerful man in Hollywood. Nobody liked to cross the Mob, so nobody was going to say no to Roselli.

This isn't to say that Monroe didn't have the talent to make it without the Mob's help, but in the beginning, when her sheer sexuality had failed to materialise on the screen, the studios didn't give her much of a chance. The director John Huston was one of the few who did see her potential. He recalled:

'I first met Marilyn in 1949 when I was filming *When We Were Strangers*, and she used to come to the set and watch the shooting. There was some talk about Columbia giving her a screen test and I had the inkling that she was being set up by someone. She was a very pretty girl, no doubt about it, and the talk I heard was that she was heading for the casting couch. I believe the couch belonged to [producer] Sam Spiegel. There was something about her that made me feel protective towards her, so to forestall her experience on the casting couch, I agreed to do a screen test of her with John Garfield. We shot it in colour, so it was not cheap to do. After that I didn't see her for a while, and forgot about her. I don't know if she did end up on that casting couch.

'When I came to do *The Asphalt Jungle*, Marilyn came to read for the part of Angela. Johnny Hyde, her agent, sent her over, and when she walked in, I recognised her as the girl I'd saved from the casting couch. At least, I hope I did! When we gave her the part, it wasn't because any hood was telling us we had to, but we gave her the part simply because she was so damned good.'

Huston told me that the person who was trying to set her up was Johnny Roselli. He was, said Huston, 'a nasty person. Everyone knew he was a gangster, but nobody told him to his face.'

The first affair between Monroe and Sinatra was brief – there was a temporary respite while Frank made various futile attempts at reconciliation with Ava. 'It was never gonna work,' Ava told me. Their divorce became final in 1957. After three disastrous marriages – first to Mickey Rooney, then Artie Shaw, then Sinatra – Ava swore she'd never wed again. In 1974 she told me, 'I still love Frank, you know. I can't live with him. But I can't live totally without him.' He obviously felt the same way, because they remained friends right up until Ava's death in 1990.

Frank moved on, although, said Huston, he never got over Ava. There were other women in Sinatra's life after her, but he never came close to feeling the same about any one of them as he did about Ava – except, perhaps, for Marilyn Monroe. Others may dispute that, citing the fact that he also remained friends with his first wife Nancy for the rest of his life. I believe, however, that he always felt a certain loyalty to Nancy, despite their bitter divorce, because she was the mother of his children. That was a different kind of bond from the one he had with Ava. They had no children to tie them together for life, but they nevertheless remained inextricably bound.

As for Marilyn Monroe, one can only speculate how their relationship would have endured had she lived. I don't think anyone believes that they would ever have stayed together, but, had she not died so young, she would, I am sure, have been another woman he would have been in love with for ever. Events would prove that he was ready to move heaven and earth for her. She also had the advantage of knowing full well that Sinatra was in league with the Mafia – because she was too. To her, like him, it was just business. Unlike Ava, she never berated him for his Mob links.

Marilyn worked again for Huston, on *The Misfits*, written by her then husband, the playwright Arthur Miller. During filming on location in Nevada in 1960, Frank Sinatra invited Huston and the entire cast to the Cal-Neva for free dinner and a show. Huston recalled, 'I remember old Joe Kennedy was also there with Jack – and so was that weasel Sam Giancana and his ass-wiper Johnny Roselli.'

By this time Marilyn was already involved sexually with Jack Kennedy. There have been some – many of them close to Monroe – who have maintained that there never was any such affair. Pat Newcomb, her personal publicist, was one. Newcomb worked for the Arthur Jacobs public relations firm. One of her associates, Rupert Allan, handled the publicity for many top stars, including Sinatra. It was Frank who persuaded Pat Newcomb to take on Marilyn's publicity. Apparently he felt that she would be the perfect person to keep an eye on the vulnerable and often unstable Marilyn.

Tony Curtis was another who insisted that Monroe had nothing to do with the Kennedys. He said, and rightly, that towards the end of her life she was an untidy, often dirty person. For that reason alone, said Curtis, neither Jack nor Bobby Kennedy would have had anything to do with her.

It may well be that Tony Curtis spoke out of loyalty to Sinatra. From as far back as 1957, when they starred together in *Kings Go Forth*, they had been friends. Over the years following her death, Tony also became loyal to the memory of Marilyn Monroe, which was a contrast to his attitude when she was alive. Joan Collins, who worked with him in the 1970 television series *The Persuaders*, told me that she couldn't stand Curtis, saying that she'd never known anyone speak about Monroe with such loathing. Even her author sister Jackie once berated Curtis on television for the criticisms he made of Marilyn.

In latter years, however, Curtis has spoken about Monroe with considerable fondness, and today he denies he ever said the classic quote, 'Kissing Marilyn Monroe was like kissing Hitler.' Unfortunately, two other people, one of them Jack Lemmon, have gone on record saying they were there, in the studio screening room watching the rushes from *Some Like It Hot*, when Tony delivered his famous line. Since then, and certainly since the early 1970s, he has clearly had a change of heart about Marilyn, and from that a certain kind of loyalty to her has evolved – and so he has publicly dismissed any suggestion that she was involved with the Kennedys.

His loyalty to Sinatra may well have coloured his views. Curtis remained close to Sinatra to the very end. In Tina Sinatra's memoir, she conjures up a poignant picture of Tony cradling her ailing father in his final months, kissing him 'as a son would his father'. She also wrote that she later discovered that, while Tony was holding Sinatra, memories of his own father's death were 'washing over him'. I have to say, based on my own experience, that Tony Curtis is one of the kindest, funniest and most gracious, Hollywood actors from a bygone age.

Despite Pat Newcomb's and Tony Curtis's denials about a relationship between Marilyn Monroe and either of the Kennedys, Peter Lawford has said differently. Since he told me about this – and everything to do with Monroe's death – under duress from Ava, I have no reason to doubt him.

There have been many who have suggested that Sinatra was responsible for arranging liaisons between Marilyn and Jack Kennedy. Certainly, Frank had been happy to pass on the phone numbers of various movie actresses to Jack, but in Marilyn's case he had nothing to do with it. Peter Lawford, who was married to Jack's and Bobby's sister Pat, said that he was solely responsible for setting his brother-in-law Jack up with Marilyn, bringing them together at parties he threw at his Santa Monica beach house.

He was later shocked to discover that his house had been wired, not only by the Mafia, but also by the FBI – and possibly the CIA It all becomes a convoluted conspiracy plot, and trying to unravel all the facts is almost impossible. What Lawford did know for sure – what he later learned – was that someone on behalf of the Mafia and one of the American secret agencies had audiotapes of Monroe and JFK making love in his beach house.

Later, after Jack had finished with Marilyn, Lawford arranged for Bobby to meet with her, and thereafter Bobby was perfectly capable of making his own arrangements to be with Marilyn, often at her home.

During the party at the Cal-Neva for the cast of *The Misfits* something occurred, apparently involving Jack Kennedy, that upset Marilyn. John Huston recalled:

'Marilyn was in a bad way. It was obvious things were bad between her and Arthur Miller. I saw him humiliated by her a number of times. She also had her hangers-on who enjoyed humiliating him. It must have been their way of proving their loyalty to Marilyn. There was one evening, after filming in the desert, when I was about to drive back, and I saw Arthur standing alone. His own wife and her friends had left him stranded there, and if I hadn't seen him, that's where he would have stayed the night – and probably died from exposure. So I have to admit I had more sympathy for him than for her.

'She was so heavily into drugs at that time. The doctor on location finally refused to give her any more, but she managed to find some elsewhere. Eventually she took an overdose and had to be rushed to hospital. Filming closed down for two weeks.

'I went to see her in hospital, and she seemed much better and I began to think we might finish the picture after all. She was bright and alert, and she said she felt guilty about her behaviour. She knew exactly what the drugs were doing to her and said to me so plaintively, "Can you forgive me?"

'I said, "You just get better."

'When she came back to work we thought it would all go better. But within a few days we knew we were over-optimistic.

She returned to her old ways, Arthur moved out of her hotel room at her request, and she went downhill. One afternoon she seemed in a kind of a trance, the worst I'd ever seen her. Her hair was a tangle, her hands and feet were dirty and the nightie she wore was filthy. But we somehow managed to finish the picture. It was agonising for all of us. Of course, it was the last film she ever completed. But she was wonderful in it.

'I believe it was some time after that she began her relationship with Frank Sinatra, and I understand that for a while she became more stable, which had a lot to do with Frank.'

In early 1961, Frank and Marilyn were an item again. She spent much of her time in New York taking acting lessons from Lee Strasberg. She made frequent visits back to the West Coast, where she dated Frank, as well as receiving treatment for her pill addiction with psychiatrist Dr Ralph Greenson. On one of these visits, Frank gave her a French poodle. She said the dog was 'my baby – mine and Frank's'. She called the poodle Maf – short for Mafia, for obvious reasons.

Dr Greenson felt that her relationship with Sinatra was not helping her treatment. She would often be several hours late for her meetings with Greenson because she was spending time with Frank at his Palm Springs home.

When Sinatra was performing at the Sands in June 1961, the audience included Peter and Pat Lawford, Eddie Fisher and Elizabeth Taylor, and Marilyn Monroe – who was very drunk. As Sinatra sang, all eyes were on Monroe as she swayed drunkenly with the music and pounded her hands on the stage, her breasts virtually pouring out of her low-cut dress.

At the party afterwards, Sinatra let her know in no uncertain terms that he was not happy about her behaviour, and Marilyn quickly left. She was, in fact, very ill, although Sinatra put it down to her inability to hold her drink. She had been suffering for more than a year with a pain in her side, but she never told Frank about it. Her physician, Dr Hyman Engelberg, had failed to diagnose the problem. Marilyn was finally hospitalised at the end of June in the Manhattan Polyclinic, where she was found to be suffering from impacted gallstones. She had immediate surgery.

In September, she flew from New York to California to attend a Democratic Party fundraiser at the Hilton Hotel with Sinatra. When he arrived in full evening dress to pick her up from her apartment, he was taken completely by surprise: for once she was ready on time. More than that, he was bowled over by the sight of her in a stunning three-thousand-dollar green sequinned dress.

They embraced, then he told her to close her eyes, and he pinned onto her ears a pair of emerald and diamond earrings. Marilyn looked in the mirror and said how beautiful they were.

'They oughta be,' said Frank. 'They cosy thirty-five thousand dollars.'

Ava said she couldn't see how Marilyn was even remotely Frank's type. He liked strong women (although Ava thought she, herself, was possibly too strong), and didn't want to have to deal with women who were generally weak and vulnerable. Yet Huston thought those were the very qualities in Monroe – as well as her stunning looks and sexual prowess – that attracted Sinatra. He understood one of her biggest weaknesses – a dependency on sleeping tablets. He'd gone through all that and had kicked the habit, although he never quit the booze. He wanted to be her protector – perhaps because he had failed to be a real father to his children, and he needed someone who could rely on him and him alone. Yet Monroe relied too heavily on too many people. Frank, it seemed, tried to make her his and his alone.

Chapter Seven

The Mob, the Kennedys – and Frank in the Middle

There have been so many misconceptions about the involvement of Frank Sinatra with regard to the links between John F Kennedy's presidential campaign and the Mafia that getting to the heart of what really happened has been a constant source of fascination for those researching that period of American history.

The general belief is that Joe Kennedy, or even JFK himself, went to Frank Sinatra and asked him to speak on their behalf to Sam Giancana to help win the Illinois vote. The way in which Giancana was best able to give his aid was to use the unions over which the Chicago Mafia had control to swing votes, and to rig the campaign with false votes, which necessitated the bribery of many law-enforcement officers in Chicago.

Sinatra himself was partly responsible for propagating the myth that he was a go-between for Giancana and the Kennedys. He told his youngest daughter, Tina, that he had been a liaison between Joe Kennedy and Sam Giancana 'on a mission that may have swung the 1960 presidential election'.

In her memoir, Tina Sinatra wrote that her father had told her he had been summoned to Hyannis Port early in 1960. He assumed he was going to be asked to sing at a fundraiser, but Joe Kennedy told him that he needed support from the Mob-run unions to get Jack into the White House. 'You and I know the same people,' Joe told Frank, 'and you know the people I mean.'

'Sure,' said Sinatra.

'I can't go to these people,' said Joe. 'It might come back at Jack. But you can. The best thing you can do for Jack is to ask for their help as a personal favour to you. Keep us out of it.'

According to Tina, Sinatra called Giancana and made a date with him to play golf. On the course, he told Sam, 'I've never come to you for a favour before, but this time I have to.' And he told Giancana what Kennedy had asked.

Sam the Cigar said, 'It's a couple of phone calls. Tell the old man I said hello.'

Yet this tale does not fit the version of events as told to me – and neither Ava Gardner, nor Peter Lawford, nor Sammy Davis Jr is around any longer for me to have the chance of going over it again with them. Perhaps it was just that Sinatra made the initial contact, and then left it between Giancana and the Kennedys to sort out. Perhaps it was just too good a story for Frank Sinatra to deny.

There was, in fact, no need for the Kennedys to ask Sinatra to be their go-between. Joe Kennedy had long had his own associations with the Mafia, having been a bootlegger in league with Frank Costello during Prohibition. He had then been busy importing the finest Scotch and Irish whiskies, as well as French champagne, distributing them from secret warehouses on the East and West Coasts. Trying to bring liquor through West Detroit without the permission of the city's Jewish Mob, known as the Purple Gang, he found himself with a contract on his life. To save himself, he went to see the Mafia boss Diamond Joe and his associates Paul Ricca and Murray Humphreys. Kennedy had to beg them to save him, and finally they agreed and were able to get the contract lifted. It was no small favour they gave: from then on Joe Kennedy was in their debt, and that meant he could not refuse them favours in return, no matter how many times they asked.

Joe Kennedy may well have got the idea of using the Mafia to sponsor his son's rise to the White House from the time when he was ordered by the Mafia to pour millions of his own money into Franklin D Roosevelt's presidential campaign. The Mob were very agreeable to supporting Roosevelt. When Roosevelt was in the White House, he appointed Joe Kennedy as chairman of the Securities and Exchange Commission, and later made him ambassador to England.

By 1956, when Frank Costello had a high standing in the Mafia, due largely to Lucky Luciano's exile from America, Joe Kennedy had again fallen foul of the Mob. Time and again Costello had asked him to return past favours, which were not forthcoming. Costello lost patience with Kennedy and put a contract on him.

In May 1956, Joe Kennedy was able to arrange for a face-to-face meeting with Sam Giancana in Chicago. Whether or not the two had met before I don't know, but this meeting did take place, as Sinatra was to discover later and relate to Ava Gardner. Kennedy asked Giancana to intercede, and when the Chicago don asked why he should do him any favours, Kennedy outlined his plan to put Jack into the White House. He promised Giancana, 'If you help me now, I'll see to it that you'll have the president's ear when he is the president.'

Giancana succeeded in having the contract on Kennedy lifted. Joe had already laid the foundation for acquiring Giancana's help to win Jack the presidency.

In 1957, Frank Costello was facing charges of tax evasion. An attempt to kill him failed, and he went on to find himself behind bars at the Atlanta Penitentiary. His successor – the man who had ordered the bodged execution – was Vito Genovese. Later that year, Genovese was also arrested and sent to the Atlanta

Penitentiary. Sam Giancana was now the most powerful Mafia boss in America.

Nonetheless, Giancana became alarmed when, in August 1957, Joe Kennedy's other son Robert was made Chief Counsel to the Senate Select Committee on Improper Activities in the Labor of Management Field. Bobby announced that his intention was to do what Edgar J Hoover had always failed to do – to investigate organised crime. His main target was Jimmy Hoffa, leader of the Teamsters Union. Although it was never proven, Hoffa was answerable to Sam Giancana. Sinatra knew that fact, and so did Bobby Kennedy.

By then Sinatra had reached a point where he felt he could throw his weight around, regardless of whatever or whomever it might affect. One New Year's Eve, Sinatra wined and dined a number of guests at his Beverly Hills home – Peter and Pat Lawford, and Robert Wagner and Natalie Wood. The plan was for them all to fly to his desert mansion, but the weather turned bad and Lawford suggested they ought to wait until morning. Pat agreed, as did Wagner and Wood.

But Sinatra simply flew into a rage, yelled, 'Well, I'm going,' and stormed out.

The party broke up and they all went home. The next morning the Lawfords returned to Sinatra's home, where he kept a special room just for them, and found that all their clothes had been thrown into the swimming pool. 'Frank liked everything done his way – to coin a phrase,' Lawford told me, 'not anyone else's.'

Sinatra had a penthouse suite at the Fontainebleau Hotel in Miami. When he decided he didn't like the furniture, instead of just having it moved out, he told his bodyguards to throw it all out. Said his former bodyguard Andy Celentano, 'One time he took a dislike to the piano. "Hey," he said, "let's toss this out the window." So me and him struggled to throw the thing out of the window. Luckily, it was too heavy to lift.'

Celentano also recalled a night when they went to a Miami club, and the first thing Sinatra did was to throw a chair across the room. 'Get rid of this,' he yelled. 'I want a high-back chair.' The manager turned up and Sinatra engaged him in such a furious argument that it almost came to blows. He ordered his bodyguards to lay into the manager, but the guards knew full well that the club had its own Mafia hit men, and refused to fight. Sinatra stormed out, swearing at his men for backing down.

In 1958 John Sturges directed Frank Sinatra in *Never So Few*. Sturges told me the following story about Sinatra and his Mob-style way of life.

When Frank arrived for filming, he invariably had men with him who, Sturges came to realise, were his personal bodyguards. 'They looked just like Mafia types to me,' he said. 'Smart suits, white shirts, dark ties.'

He asked Sinatra if these men were actual Mafia.

'Nah!' replied Sinatra. 'These guys belong to me.'

'What do you need them for?'

'To stop me getting killed.'

'Who's gonna kill you, Frank?'

'You never know.'

'Look, Frank, I know you've got your friends in high and low places, but I don't want any gangland-style shooting on my picture.'

'That ain't gonna happen.'

'And how can you be sure?'

'Because I got my guys with me.'

This perplexed Sturges, who said, 'But doesn't the fact that you've got your bodyguards with you mean that you expect trouble?'

'John, believe me when I say that where I go, trouble may

follow, and these guys make sure it never catches up.'

'Okay, Frank, but you'll forgive me if I say that if we get any trouble because you're having to look over your shoulder, there'll be hell to pay.'

'Relax, John. The fact I got these guys means there'll be no trouble. They do the looking over my shoulder for me.'

Sturges had the feeling that Sinatra felt vulnerable without his own little Mafia, but he never knew why Frank needed such strong-arm protection. Sturges even had words with Peter Lawford, who was also in the picture, and asked, 'Why does Frank have those guys in black with him?'

'Oh, that's just Frank's way of letting everyone know he won't be screwed with.'

Sturges never did get a proper answer to his question. He told me, 'Maybe it was just to keep the reporters and cameramen in their place. Or maybe something more sinister. Either way, there was no trouble, and I got on with Sinatra okay.'

Sam Giancana was, to put it mildly, nonplussed at having saved Joe Kennedy's life only to find his associates being summoned by Bobby Kennedy to appear before the McClellan Committee in 1959. As he saw it, Joe Kennedy had betrayed him. Ava recalled, 'Frank always said that Joe Kennedy was the biggest gangster of them all. You never turned your back on him.'

Either through sheer audacity or a certain naivety, Joe Kennedy met with Giancana in Chicago at around this time, to establish an understanding with regard to his quest to get Jack the presidency with the help of the Mafia. Giancana was not slow to come to the point, and asked what Bobby was doing trying to prove a connection between the Teamsters Union and some of his own associates.

Joe Kennedy told him, 'You've no need to worry, Sam. Nothing Bobby does will affect you.'

Giancana wasn't convinced: he, like Sinatra, didn't trust Joe. Yet he went along with the plan, and there were discussions between Joe Kennedy and Sam Giancana in the first few months of 1959 to establish a plan of action. Because of his distrust of Kennedy, Giancana also quickly set in motion a plan to ensure that, if Joe betrayed him, the Kennedys would all go down together. He knew that Jack and Bobby had inherited their father's greatest weakness: women. He would set sexual traps for Jack and Bobby and, if the time came, he'd blow the whistle on them both.

Unwittingly caught up in this conspiracy was Frank Sinatra. Both Ava and Lawford were adamant that Sinatra's role in all this was at the most minimal. According to C David Heymann's biography of Robert Kennedy, there were certainly 'associates' who intervened to bring Joe Kennedy and Sam Giancana together for their initial meeting, but that book makes no mention of Sinatra being a part of that.

As Ava told it, it was Giancana who called on Frank to get involved with JFK's presidential campaign: Joe Kennedy had been perfectly capable of allying himself with Giancana without Sinatra's help. To Giancana, Sinatra was the perfect foil, because not only was he arguably the greatest entertainer in America who could influence citizens to vote for Jack, but Sam also knew he could make use of his latest business venture with Sinatra.

Giancana knew that the Kennedys, including Joe, enjoyed spending time at a nightclub at Lake Tahoe – the Cal-Neva Lodge. Sam bought the place, and made Frank Sinatra a part-owner, along with Skinny D'Amato. Giancana remained a silent partner. It would be the perfect place to provide a private bungalow, complete with bugging devices and girls for Jack and Bobby Kennedy to enjoy.

There were occasions when Joe Kennedy personally met Sam Giancana at the Cal-Neva. It has been suggested that Sinatra carried messages back and forth between Joe and Sam, but, with Joe Kennedy fraternising so closely with Giancana, there would seem little point in Sinatra agreeing to play the meagre part of a messenger.

If it is true that Frank participated in the plans drawn up between Giancana and Joe Kennedy, I am convinced he could only have played a minimal part – hardly more than a social conversation here and there. He was certainly not a major player in any real sense. His major role was that of a celebrity openly supporting JFK for the presidency.

For Sinatra, the chance of becoming a close confidant of a future president was irresistible to his ego and vanity, and that was enough for him to get involved. He also said, according to both Ava Gardner and Peter Lawford, that he supported Jack because he thought he was 'the right man for the job'. He certainly knew that Giancana had promised his own support to the campaign, and that didn't hurt Sinatra at all.

But, said Ava, Frank had no idea that Giancana was going to use the Cal-Neva as a place to dig the dirt on the Kennedys. Frank would never have stood for that, she said. She also pointed out that Frank had access to the Kennedy fold even without having to be persuaded by Giancana, given that his fellow Rat Packer Peter Lawford was married to Patricia Kennedy, daughter of Joe.

Chapter Eight

From Rat Pack to Jack Pack

Peter Lawford seemed, from the very beginning, an unlikely candidate for membership of the so-called 'Rat Pack'. He was not a singer, or even a comedian, but simply a British actor. The illegitimate son of a knighted British general, Peter was born on 7 September 1923 in London, and was educated in private schools in England. He made his screen debut at the age of just eight in a 1931 British film, *Poor Old Bill*. In 1938 he was taken on a visit to California, where he came to the attention of Metro-Goldwyn-Mayer, who cast the young, upper-class English teenager as a Cockney lad in *Lord Jeff*. Louis B Mayer decided to put Peter under contract and launched him as their brightest new star in 1942, in small roles in prestige picture such as *Mrs Miniver* and *Random Harvest*. He was given his first starring role in 1945 in *Son of Lassie*, and was then co-starred in a series of films opposite the studio's top leading ladies, Judy Garland, June Allyson and Elizabeth Taylor.

In 1945, at a party thrown by the studio boss Louis B Mayer, Lawford met MGM's latest acquisition, Frank Sinatra. Frank was 29, Peter 22. They were the youngest people at the party. Lawford said, 'Frank was a twenty-nine-year-old bobbysox idol with hollow cheeks who could talk with his fists. He was a tough little Italian son of a bitch, and for some reason that persona appealed to me. We made a strange combination, with me being the ever-so-ever-so son of a British Knight of the Realm, and him with his brash, cocky and often arrogant attitude and friends in the Mafia. But we hit it off.'

Lawford also hit it off with Ava Gardner, and for a while they enjoyed a brief fling, but, after Ava married Sinatra, Lawford steered well clear of any amorous encounters with her. Following the break-up of the marriage, Lawford met up with Ava for a drink upon her return from working overseas. As they talked over old times and laughed together, they were spotted by the gossip columnist Louella Parson. The next day her column proclaimed, 'Ava's first date back in the U.S. is Peter Lawford.'

Lawford told me, 'At three o'clock the next morning I was awakened by Sinatra calling me on the phone and yelling, "What the fuck are you doing going out with Ava? You want both your legs broken?"

'I tried to explain we were just having a drink, but he wouldn't listen. He didn't speak to me for about five years.'

Lawford was bitter about his expulsion by Sinatra. Then, in 1959, Frank suddenly welcomed him back into the gang when they met up at a dinner party thrown by Gary Cooper. 'We spoke as though the past five years had never happened,' said Lawford. He claimed that, although he didn't realise it then, Sinatra was simply using the Lawfords as a way of ingratiating himself with the Kennedys.

Ava maintained that she didn't know if that was true or not, but she insisted that, if Frank hadn't been genuinely fond of Peter, he would never have got involved with him again, even for the sake of the Kennedys.

What was certain, to both Ava and Lawford, was that Frank could not have foreseen what lay ahead.

Meanwhile, Sinatra had made Jack Kennedy his new best friend

– or perhaps it was Jack Kennedy who made Sinatra his new best friend. Whichever way it worked, Sinatra maintained the friendship by introducing Jack to a number of female movie stars.

After years of journalists and researchers desperate to prove that Jack and Bobby Kennedy were in league with the Mafia, there arose the misconception that Jack and Bobby knew all about and approved of Sam Giancana's support. This was not strictly the case. While Joe Kennedy was making promises to Giancana that he had nothing to fear from Bobby's investigation into organised crime, Bobby finally summoned Giancana himself to appear before the McClellan Committee in June 1959.

Some of the exchanges between Bobby Kennedy and Sam Giancana have become legend, and show that there was absolutely no rapport or secret agreement between them at all.

Bobby asked, 'Would you tell us – if you have any opposition from anybody – you dispose of them by having them stuffed in a trunk? Is that what you do, Mr Giancana?'

Giancana chuckled and said, as he had done some 34 times during the hearing, 'I decline to answer because I honestly believe my answer may incriminate me.'

'Can you tell us anything about any of your operations, or are you just going to giggle every time I ask you a question?'

'I decline to answer because I honestly believe my answer may incriminate me.'

'I thought only little girls giggled, Mr Giancana.'

Despite all this, Giancana maintained his support for Jack's race to the White House. Why? Some have speculated that Bobby's putting Giancana on show and berating him with questions about his alleged Mob involvement was all a sham. Sinatra never believed that. He was nervous about his own name coming up once more, as it had done at the time of the Kefauver hearings, and he felt helpless as he watched this latest televised debate on the Mafia.

What he would later learn was that the Kennedy brothers, desperate to clean up the family act as far as their father's links to the Mafia were concerned, were never going to implicate Sinatra, if only because his involvement in the presidential campaign was purely legitimate. Sinatra had been a lifelong Democrat, and Jack Kennedy was his natural choice. All he had to do was appear at Democratic rallies with his Rat Pack, do a little entertaining, and attempt to influence votes.

The man behind all the wheeling and dealing with the Mob was Joe Kennedy. At precisely which point the Kennedy brothers discovered this, neither Sinatra nor Lawford knew. Neither Jack nor Bobby approved of the Mafia, and they were going to prove it – but they had to do it without hurting their father. They knew that the best way to do this was first to get into the White House, and then for Jack to install Bobby as attorney general. They were also anxious to try to get J Edgar Hoover out of the FBI. Both Sinatra and Lawford believed that knowledge of Joe's dealings with Giancana came to Jack and Bobby only after Bobby had questioned Giancana. That's when Joe would have told them, and thereafter Bobby had to lay off Giancana – but he intended to do so only for a while, until Jack was president.

Joe assured Giancana that he would not be interrogated by Bobby again, and the Mafia-sponsored campaign continued. Jack even had to meet with Giancana, accompanied by his father, at Chicago's Ambassador East towards the end of 1959, to promise him that Bobby would take the heat off the Mob. Jack knew, however, that it was a promise he would not keep.

Even if Frank Sinatra had been inclined to be involved in Joe Kennedy's and Sam Giancana's vote rigging, he was too busy. He was also trying to sort out a new recording deal, having decided to finish with Capitol Records because, he felt, they were restricting him in the way he wanted to record his music.

By this time the famous Rat Pack had come into being, consisting mainly of Sinatra, Lawford, Dean Martin, Sammy Davis Jr and Joey Bishop. Sinatra hated the term 'Rat Pack'. In fact, the Rat Pack didn't begin with him. It may have become famous as 'Sinatra's Rat Pack', but initially it was really Humphrey Bogart's Rat Pack.

Its beginnings were as far back as 1941, when Humphrey Bogart and wife Lauren 'Betty' Bacall used to entertain a group of friends, which included David Niven and his wife Hjordis, Spencer Tracy, the writer Nunally Johnson, Gloria Grahame and John Huston, to name just a few. It happened just by accident. Bogie and Betty were gaining a reputation for throwing the best parties in Hollywood, and people just wanted to be there. But the Bogarts always had their own favourite friends who all had one thing in common: they detested the Hollywood studio star system. They all fought against studio heads, and gained the reputation for being difficult. It wasn't so much that they *were* difficult – they were just tough to deal with. They preferred to tell the studio heads what *they* wanted to do.

Into this select group was welcomed Frank Sinatra in 1953. Lauren Bacall said, 'I don't remember how the friendship with Frank began, but he was alone and not happy because neither his work nor his personal life had been going well. So we had dinner with him a few times.'

In January 1954, Bogie had to leave for Rome to make *The Barefoot Contessa* with Ava Gardner. Bacall went to New York for a while and planned to head for London and then go on to Rome. Before she left for London, Sinatra called her and asked if she would take a coconut cake to Ava. 'Apparently, she liked coconut cake,' said Bacall. She knew that things had not been going well between Frank and Ava during what was one of their many attempts at reconciliation, and this was his way of trying to mend romantic fences.

The cake arrived at Bacall's house and she personally carried it by hand all the way to London, and then to Rome, to prevent it from getting crushed. When she arrived at the Excelsior Hotel where she would be staying with Bogie, she asked him if he would tell Ava that there was a cake waiting for her.

'She did nothing about it,' recalled Bacall. 'So two days later I decided to take it to her dressing room at the studio before the cake rotted.'

She didn't know Ava and said she felt very awkward, because 'who knows what has happened between a man and a woman when it goes sour?' She said she 'felt like an idiot, standing there with the bloody box'.

She told Ava, 'I brought this cake for you. Frank sent it to me in New York. He thought you'd like it.'

Ava told her to put it down on the table 'without so much as a thank you', said Bacall. 'She couldn't have cared less. She was in love with a bullfighter named Luis Miguel Dominguin. I stood there, very much out of place, and finally managed to get away. I was furious with her. I never told Frank the coconut cake saga: he would have been too hurt.'

When she told Bogie about it, he said, 'That's the thing with the girls at MGM. They're so pampered, so catered for, they're totally spoiled and self-indulgent. But she's professional about her work and that's all I care about.'

Bogie liked Sinatra, and when the marriage to Ava came to a definite end, the Bogarts took it upon themselves to befriend Frank by inviting him over to dinner and to join in with their parties. John Huston, one of the Bogart regulars, told me, 'Frank was a lonely guy, still in love with Ava, who was probably the only woman who ever left him.'

Sinatra had a great fondness for Bogie and Spencer Tracy. Being with them, said Bacall, gave him 'a feeling of solidarity that his life lacked. He really came alive at night, due to a lifetime of training as a band singer.'

The Bogarts had developed a secret signal for privileged callers: if their light was on over the front door, their special friends were welcome to join them for a drink. Sinatra was turning up there almost every night, even after late engagements. One night, Bogie told Lauren, 'You don't think he comes to see *me*, do you? You're the attraction.' Bacall said that Bogie 'sold himself short' and she was not the only attraction for Frank's regular visits.

This close-knit Bogart clan became known as the Rat Pack. David Niven once explained how the name came about:

'Noël Coward was appearing in Las Vegas at the Desert Inn. Frank Sinatra invited a few friends to go with him to Las Vegas for the opening. The group consisted of Betty and Bogie, Mike and Gloria Romanoff, Ernie Kovaks and his wife, Swifty Lazar, Sid Luft and Judy Garland, Angie Dickinson, my wife Hjordis, and myself.

'When Sinatra organises anything, the arrangements are made with legendary efficiency, not to mention generosity. We all boarded a bus outside Bogie's front door. There was caviar and champagne to sustain us during the drive to the Union Station, where, with a cry from our leader [Sinatra] of 'yellow armbands, follow me,' we marched on to the train and into a private coach for the overnight trip.

'Sinatra provided individual apartments for everyone at the Sands Hotel, as well as a large communal suite with hot and cold running food and drink twenty-four hours a day. A big bag of silver dollars was presented to each girl in the group.

'We watched Noël's triumphant first night and then on the other evenings we visited all the other shows in Las Vegas. We all gambled endlessly, and it all began to get very tiring. After three days of this, Judy Garland slipped me something that she said would keep me going. It was the size of a horse-pill, inside of which were dozens of little energy nuggets which were timed to go off at forty-minute intervals.

'After four days and nights of complete self-indulgence, the only one of us who seemed physically untouched by it all was Frank Sinatra, while the rest of us were wrecks. It was then that Betty Bacall surveyed the bedraggled group, and said, "You lot look like a goddam Rat Pack!"'

'A week later, we returned to Los Angeles and some semblance of normality. The Rat Pack threw a testimonial dinner to Frank in a private room at Romanoff's, where we were welcomed with a surprise package, tied with pink ribbon and flown down especially by Jack Entratta, who was the entrepreneur of the Sands Hotel. We opened our packages and we each found a white rat. During the unpacking, several escaped and, running throughout the restaurant, created instant alarm among the chic clientele, among whom were some eagle-eyed columnists who made a point of finding out what was going on – and thus was heralded the existence of Frank Sinatra's Rat Pack.'

To join the Rat Pack, said Bacall, 'one had to be addicted to nonconformity, staying up late, drinking, laughing, and not caring what anyone thought or said about us'.

The Rat Pack had a varying group of members. Most of the time it was made up of Judy Garland and her husband Sid Luft, agent Swifty Lazar, the Nivens, Spencer Tracy, Mike Romanoff and his wife, Betty and Bogie, and Sinatra – as well as Bogie's great friend John Huston, who said, 'I was only a part-time member of the Rat Pack.'

While Bogie was the undisputed head of the Rat Pack, he proclaimed Frank Sinatra the president. The Rat Packers rarely frequented Las Vegas, but Frank insisted they become his guests at the Sands Hotel, where he was now performing regularly. 'He really enjoyed being head man,' said Bacall, 'arranging everything in his territory.' He arranged for the Pack to have the front tables for the show, dinner, drinks, and a hundred dollars' worth of chips each for the gambling tables.

As Huston noted, 'Frank was also serving his masters in the Mob, because he knew a hundred dollars wouldn't be enough for the Rat Packers to play with, and so they spent plenty of money at the tables.'

Bogart knew that he and the others should not get too embroiled in Sinatra's rather lonely bachelor existence. On New Year's Eve 1955, the Rat Pack went to Sinatra's Palm Springs home, but most of the party had made arrangements that prevented them from staying over. Frank begged the Bogarts to stay.

'He looked very forlorn and alone,' recalled Bacall. Bogie knew she felt they should stay, but he said to Frank, 'Sorry, pal, we've got to get back to town.'

On the way back to Los Angeles, Bacall told Bogie, 'We should have stayed.'

Bogie replied, 'No, we shouldn't. We have a life of our own that has nothing to do with Frank. He chose to live alone. It's too bad if he's lonely, but that's his choice. We can't live his life.'

When Bogie fell ill with lung cancer, Frank was among those who visited frequently. 'During the last months of Bogie's illness,' recalled Bacall, 'Frank was away working off and on. If he was in town, he came over at least twice a week. When he couldn't come, he never failed to call by phone. Towards the end, he seemed to be instinctively there at key moments. I guess I began to depend on his presence or his voice at the other end of the phone.'

When Bogie died in 1957, Sinatra was distraught that his work kept him away from the funeral, but he called Lauren by phone several times. She finally accepted his invitation to get away by spending two weeks at his house in Palm Springs. She took their children and her mother with her, and Frank made sure he was absent to allow them to grieve.

In time, Bacall and Sinatra briefly became an item, although Bacall said she could never remember how it all began. It didn't work out between them. She found she was seeing less of Frank than she had done when she had Bogie. She explained, 'I really didn't know where I stood with Frank. I never understood the love game. I expected him to call or to see him every night. But Frank liked to be kept off balance. I was the wrong girl for that.' The warmth that Bacall had felt for Sinatra while she was married to Bogie cooled off when she fell for him.

John Huston observed all this and told me, 'The trouble with Frank was he couldn't just be in love and devote himself to a single woman. Betty Bacall was a one-man woman, and saw a relationship as a two-way thing, with give and take. Frank became a changed man to her because he stopped giving, and only took. He couldn't give up his bachelor life and there were still the pals he had to see and the women he had to lay.

'I'm sure there was also the problem Ava had had with Frank – with his Mob buddies. Betty would be too much of a lady to talk about it publicly, but she would not have approved of his Mafia connections. She had met real gangsters because Bogie had attracted them, as did any of the stars who played gangsters, like James Cagney. That didn't mean Bogie or Cagney got to like and befriend any of them. But for Frank, some of his best friends were Mafia, and I'm positive that Betty did not approve of that at all.'

With Bogie dead, and Sinatra and Bacall now ex-lovers, the original Rat Pack broke up. Still, from then on, anyone associated with Sinatra became a part of the so-called Rat Pack.

In 1958 Sinatra made *Kings Go Forth* with Tony Curtis. For a while Curtis and his actress wife Janet Leigh were regularly partying with the Rat Pack. One night he and Janet, then pregnant with Jamie Lee, were with Sinatra and numerous others – Dean Martin, Sammy Cahn, David and Patricia North – partying at

Peter Lawford's Santa Monica beach house.

When the party was over, Tony and Janet piled into a car along with Dean Martin and Sammy Cahn, and drove off. The Norths followed in the next car, and bringing up the rear was Sinatra.

Suddenly the Norths' car was rammed by a man who seemed to believe that his fast-and-loose wife was hiding in it. His car bounced off theirs and hit the vehicle in front. Janet Leigh became hysterical, fearful for her unborn baby, and she began screaming. Curtis, Martin and Cahn tried to calm her down, while Sinatra got on his car radio and called for the police and an ambulance.

When the ambulance arrived to take her away, Curtis, Martin and Cahn held the demented driver while Sinatra stood in his car and yelled 'Mayday! Mayday!' as the police approached.

Curtis enjoyed his membership of the Rat Pack only for a brief time. He told me, 'It was terrific. I felt like a man. To be included in this circle was a wonderful feeling for me. But I didn't feel comfortable for some reason.' He made his excuses and cancelled his membership.

The Rat Pack was growing smaller and more exclusive. Dean Martin, a relative newcomer, was still a key member. Born Dino Paul Crocetti on 7 June 1917 in Steubenville, Ohio, he tried out various careers in his early days – he was a prizefighter, a steel mill labourer, and a so-called 'professional gambler'. In fact, he was a cardsharp and a small-time gangster. He could also sing, and around 1936 he began singing in night spots in his home town and later in other parts of America. In places like New York, his usual venues were Chinese restaurants or small-time clubs. His career seemed to be going nowhere.

In the spring of 1946, Dean's friend and singing companion Sonny King happened to introduce Martin to a young Jewish comedian, nineteen-year-old Jerry Lewis. The only thing Martin and Lewis had in common was that their careers seemed to be going nowhere fast.

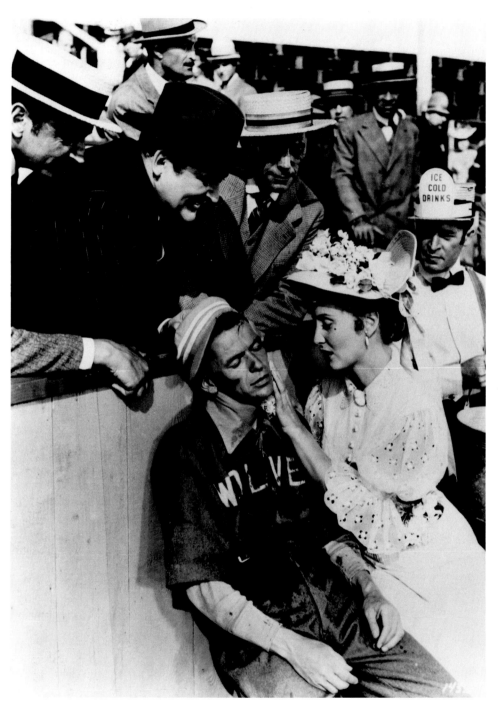

He may have looked like a puny weakling in MGM's 1949 musical *Take Me Out To The Ball Game*, but away from the studio Sinatra was already developing his own tough-guy Mob-style life. © MGM/UA

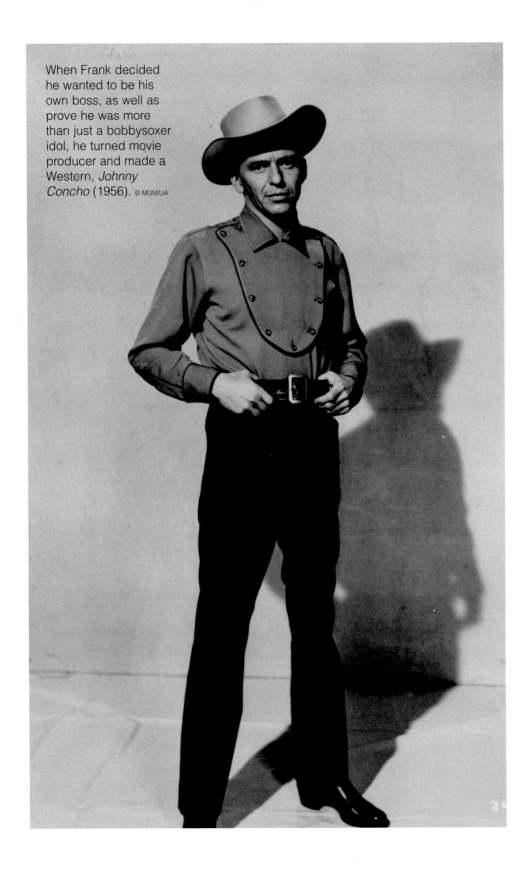

When Frank decided he wanted to be his own boss, as well as prove he was more than just a bobbysoxer idol, he turned movie producer and made a Western, *Johnny Concho* (1956). © MGM/UA

Inspired perhaps by his own business links with gangsters, Sinatra portrayed nightclub singer Joe E Lewis (who had his own run in with gangsters) in *The Joker Is Wild* (1957). He is seen here with Mitzi Gaynor. © Paramount-Viacom Inc.

Sinatra, the recording star. His relaxed, easy-going charm was at odds with his often tempestuous nature and his links to organised crime.

Sinatra didn't serve in the war but made up for it by playing a heroic GI in *Kings Go Forth* in 1957. © MGM/UA

Sinatra tried his hand at light comedy in 1959 in *A Hole In The Head*, seen here with Keenan Wynn. © Paramount-Viacom Inc.

The last studio portrait of Marilyn Monroe from the unfinished *Something's Gotta Give*. Sinatra had decided to marry her for her own protection – but she died under circumstances that led to Sinatra's vendetta against Mafia boss Sam Giancana.
© 20th Century Fox

Ava Gardner, Sinatra's ex-wife and lifelong confidante, is seen here during early days of filming *55 Days At Peking* with Charlton Heston – but after she got a call midway through production telling her that Marilyn was dead, her smile vanished for the duration. © Warner Bros.

By 1962, when Sinatra made *Come Blow Your Horn* with Lee J Cobb, he was beginning to mellow and shake off not only his connections to the Mob, but also his own Mob-style tactics, making his film sets happier places than they had been during the 1950s. © Paramount-Viacom Inc.

The Rat Pack were back on screen – minus the exiled Peter Lawford – for *Robin And The Seven Hoods* (1964). Few realised that this was Sinatra's way of thumbing his nose at the Mob. © Warner Bros.

Determined to be his own man, Sinatra directed *None But The Brave* in 1964. This was a time when he kept himself busy with movies, many of them shot abroad, to avoid contact with Sam Giancana. © Warner Bros.

In 1964, Frank was in Italy making *Von Ryan's Express* (right) at the same time as Ava was there to film John Huston's *The Bible . . . In The Beginning* (below). When Frank heard that Ava's co-star and lover George C Scott was beating her, Sinatra arranged for two Mafia-type bodyguards to watch over her and keep Scott at bay.

Sinatra's film work in the late 1960s continued at a pace. Here he's with Virna Lisi in *Assault On A Queen*. © Paramount-Viacom Inc.

Frank Sinatra of the mid-1960s. He had reason to look pleased: he'd helped to put Sam Giancana behind bars and, a little later, into exile

In 1970, Sinatra and Count Basie performed a charity concert for the National Society for the Prevention of Cruelty to Children in London, attended by the Earl of Snowdon, whose wife, Princess Margaret, was the president of the society.

The Rat Pack were back before the movie cameras one last time in 1983, with Shirley MacLaine – standing where Peter Lawford once stood – for *The Cannonball Run II*. © Warner Bros.

Sinatra, circa late 1960s, looking more like the tough guy he had once been, but underneath it all he was a more mellow, thoughtful man looking for his own redemption.

In July 1946 Dean landed in Atlantic City, where Paul 'Skinny' D'Amato was prepared to give him the biggest break of his life – playing the 500 Club. It just so happened that Jerry Lewis had just played a week there when Dean arrived. Lewis had not been a success, and he was literally packing his things to move out of his dressing room just as Dean Martin was opening on his first night. Backstage, Lewis dropped everything he was struggling to carry, and the sound carried through to the club.

'I guess Jerry's packing all his records,' joked Dean. Incensed, Lewis strode onto the stage, telling him, 'I don't think that's very nice of you,' and suddenly the audience were in hysterics. Realising something was happening to them, Martin and Lewis ad-libbed their way through a comedy act, and afterwards D'Amato told them that if they knew what was right for themselves, they'd get together as a double act. They did, and they played to packed houses and long queues at the 500 Club for the next few weeks. That started their career as a team.

Early in 1948 Skinny D'Amato, eager to show off his own various protégés, put on a show at the Copacabana in New York, featuring Frank Sinatra, Jackie Gleason, Fat Jackie Leonard, Jerry Lewis and Dean Martin. The five entertainers brought the house down, and all seemed to defer to Sinatra – except Dean Martin. It was as though he didn't know, or care, who Frank Sinatra was. This only served to fascinate Frank, who took an instant liking to Dean.

Martin and Lewis really hit the big time when they began making a series of hugely successful films together in 1948. Lewis was the funny man, Martin the straight guy. In 1956, when they made their last of sixteen films together, *Hollywood or Bust*, Martin decided to call it a day and go solo. By 1958 he had been written off. Critics and Hollywood gurus predicted that Lewis would go on being a star while Martin would soon be forgotten. Sinatra made sure he wasn't, and gave him a good role in the film

Some Came Running. The heavy-drinking crooner became as close to Frank as anyone could – apart from Sammy Davis Jr.

Sammy Davis Jr had been rescued from obscurity by Sinatra, and Sammy was forever grateful. Born on 8 December 1925 in New York, he was performing from the age of four as a novelty turn in his father's vaudeville dance routine. 'When the child-labour inspectors came snooping around,' he told me, 'I just clamped a cigar between my teeth and pretended I was a 45-year-old midget.'

In 1942 Davis was drafted into the army, where he was subjected to beatings just for being black. 'I must have had a fight every two days. That's why my nose ended up flat against my face.'

After the war he returned to the stage but refused to submit to performing Al Jolson caricatures or playing the stereotypical submissive Negro. He performed with his father and uncle as the Will Martin Trio, usually in hotels where black people were able to perform but were barred from staying the night in any of the rooms. A chance meeting with Frank Sinatra changed his fortunes, and in 1947 Sinatra had the Will Martin Trio open for him at the Capitol Theater in New York. They were paid 1,250 dollars a week. 'That was more money than we'd ever seen in our lives,' said Sammy.

Thanks to Frank, doors that had previously been closed to blacks were opened for Sammy. 'Frank knew all about intolerance. He'd been called a wop and I was called a coon. Before meeting him, I was just another black entertainer. He gave me the key.'

In 1951 Sammy, his father and uncle played at Ciro's, Hollywood's top nightclub. Sammy was the undoubted star of the trio, and the audience let him know it. After that, he began appearing on all the big television variety shows, solo, as Sammy Davis Jr.

On 19 November 1954, after finishing his last show at the New

Frontier in Las Vegas, Sammy got in his car and headed for Los Angeles. A car hit him head on, and he lost his left eye in the accident. After Sammy spent some time in hospital, Frank drove from Los Angeles to collect him and take him back to his Palm Springs home to recuperate. 'All I knew was, I never wanted to be seen in public again,' Sammy told me.

Finally, Frank said to him, 'You can sit around feeling sorry for yourself for the rest of your life, but you can kiss your career goodbye.'

Just eight weeks after the accident, Sammy was playing to a packed audience at Ciro's, wearing an eye patch. Within a year he was back in Vegas, playing a two-week engagement at the New Frontier. On the opening night he removed his eye patch on stage – and received a standing ovation.

Sammy always credited Frank with having saved his career, and he never forgot it. Ava said, 'I think Francis always loved Sammy the most in the Pack. He thought of him as a young brother he could look out for. And he trusted Sammy with his life.'

Sinatra also took a liking to the comedian Joey Bishop. He was born Joseph Abraham Gottlieb on 3 February 1918 in the Bronx in New York, although he grew up in Philadelphia, where he graduated from high school and formed the Bishop Brothers Trio with two friends. He went on to enjoy a modest nightclub career before serving in the US Army during the war. During the 1950s he became a popular television personality, starring in his own situation comedy, and he also became a friend of Sinatra and a member of the Rat Pack.

Frank preferred to call his little clan – of Davis, Martin, Bishop and himself – the Summit. He made Jack Kennedy an honorary member of the Summit, and early in 1959 he joked that his own Rat Pack had become the Jack Pack. There is no doubt that Jack Kennedy liked Sinatra and enjoyed their friendship – and not just because Frank was able to introduce him to some of the most beautiful actresses in Hollywood. There was a genuine fondness between the two men.

In January 1960 the Summit were having a ball, entertaining night after night at the Sands Hotel to packed audiences. It became the most celebrated show in town, and Sinatra personally invited Jack Kennedy to see the show and put him up in the hotel's best suite – all on the house.

While they performed at the Sands by night, they worked by day on a movie, *Ocean's Eleven*, filmed entirely in Las Vegas. As Sammy Davis said, 'You couldn't have unlimited access to Las Vegas without the – shall we say – authorisation of the Mob, and so if you want to say that Frank had associations with the Mob, it was so he could do the work he wanted to do. That means, any entertainer who worked in Las Vegas was associated with the Mob. That's just the way it was.'

Sammy Davis stated categorically that Sinatra was not involved in the deal between Joe Kennedy and Sam Giancana to rig the voting in favour of Jack. Like Ava Gardner and Peter Lawford, Sammy Davis said that, when Frank supported Jack Kennedy, 'it was because he thought he was the right man for the job'.

What Sinatra was best able to do for Kennedy's presidential campaign was simply to use his own celebrity status, which, in turn, encouraged scores of other celebrities to join in and so generated significant financial contributions to the campaign. At the request of Joe Kennedy, Sinatra was able to raise a considerable fund from among his personal friends in the movie and music business. Joe also wanted Sinatra to record a campaign theme song, and Frank chose 'High Hopes', with the lyrics specially written by the song's original lyricist, Sammy Cahn. By Election Day in 1960, that song had been played all along the campaign trail and was a popular choise on jukeboxes every-where. Sinatra was, in fact, responsible for turning a presidential campaign into a highly publicised media event. He made President Kennedy a media star, even before he was elected.

The night before Kennedy was inaugurated on 20 January 1961, Sinatra and Lawford personally organised a presidential gala that included stars such as Ella Fitzgerald, Leonard Bernstein, Nat King Cole, Tony Curtis, Janet Leigh, Angie Dickinson, Gene Kelly, Laurence Olivier and Harry Belafonte. Frank, rightly, felt he had played a huge part in getting Jack the presidency, and he was celebrating his own success as well as that of the new president.

Once in the White House, Jack Kennedy often called Sinatra on the phone, just to talk. Peter Lawford recalled:

'One night when we were having a private dinner with the president, he said, "I really ought to do something special for Frank for all he did for me. I'll ask him to the White House." Jack was really appreciative of what Frank had done to help him with the presidency.

'I told Jack: "Frank would love that."

'But Jack said, "There's just one problem. Jackie hates him. She won't entertain the idea of having him at the White House. I know. I'll wait till she goes to Middleburg and have him over then."

'Frank was over the moon when he got the call from Jack's secretary, inviting him over. He flew out to Washington [in September 1961], where a car picked him up. Jack didn't dare allow Frank to come in through the front door and have all the reporters seeing him going in and then Jackie finding out about it in the newspapers, so he was driven to the southwest gate.

'Frank always wanted to fly in Air Force One, but that was out of the question. And he was never invited to state dinners or to Camp David. But he got given a tour of the White House by Jack, and had Bloody Marys on the Truman Balcony. He loved every moment of it, and the next day he joined Pat and Ted

[Kennedy], and flew on the Kennedys' private plane to Hyannis.'

The day after the trip to Hyannis, Frank joined the president and other members of the family for a cruise on the *Honey Fitz*, the Kennedys' private yacht. Sinatra had recently returned from Italy, where he'd had a meeting with the Pope, and he told the president all about it. Like Monroe, he began calling Jack 'Prez'.

Sinatra's associations with Sam Giancana meant that the rest of the Summit got to know Sam the Cigar well. Sammy Davis once made a big mistake in asking Giancana for a loan of 23,000 dollars. He told me, 'I should have known better, but at the time I needed the money and asked Mooney. When Frank found out he yelled, "What the hell did you ask him for? You could've asked me!" But I always felt Frank had done more than enough for me already. After that loan, I owed Giancana more than just the repayment of the money.'

Davis was performing at an Atlantic City nightclub when Giancana's brother Chuck and an associate turned up to demand the money back. Davis was so terrified at the very sight of them, he paid up straight away.

Having contact with Giancana also had its advantages. When Davis began dating Kim Novak, her boss at Columbia Pictures, Harry Cohn, put a contract on him. The first Davis knew about it was when he read an article in a newspaper which said, 'Sammy Davis Jr has been warned by top Chicago gangsters that if he ever sees that blonde movie star again, both his legs will be broken and torn off from the knee.' Cohn had been responsible for ensuring that the article was published.

Davis got on the phone to 'Doctor Goldberg' and asked, 'Am I in trouble with you guys?'

'No,' replied Giancana, 'and if you were, you know I'd handle it for you.'

Feeling moderately reassured, Davis stopped dating Novak. It didn't stop Cohn. Somehow, a friend of Sammy's who was 'well connected' – as he put it in his autobiography – came to see him in his Las Vegas dressing room and said, 'Sam, you've got a problem with the guys.'

Davis said, 'No, it's okay, I talked to Sam in Chicago. That was just phoney shit in the columns.'

'I'm not talking Chicago. I'm talking Los Angeles. Harry Cohn's mad and he's got a contract out on you.'

His 'well-connected' friend assured him that in Las Vegas, Chicago and New York, they could protect him, but he warned him, 'Don't go to LA unless you straighten things out with Cohn.'

Davis thought he already had, but, just to make sure, he hastily married a black girl, Loray White, and Cohn called off the dogs. The marriage was short-lived, and in November 1960 Sammy married a woman he loved, the Swedish actress Mae Britt.

Davis himself told me in 1974 that it was Frank who warned him that one of the studio bosses was going to get him maimed – or even killed – just because he was seeing a white movie star. It was Frank who suggested that Sammy get himself married to a black girl. Meanwhile, Frank made sure Davis was safe until he knew for certain that the contract had been cancelled. As Davis said, 'That was the kind of influence Frank had with men like Mooney.' He also said that he didn't know of any time when Frank had used the Mob to do damage to anyone, but he did use the Mob to prevent damage being done to one of his friends. He also said, 'Frank could take care of most people he didn't like on his own. He was no gangster, despite the rumours, but he knew how to be one.'

Peter Lawford had instigated the friendship between Sinatra and Jack Kennedy. Sometime after Jack gained the presidency, however, that friendship seems to have started to cool. Lawford knew why: Sinatra, because of his association with Giancana, was becoming a liability to the Kennedys. It wasn't a matter of disliking Sinatra, but purely a matter of politics. J Edgar Hoover may have been turning a blind eye to the Mafia's activities and even their very existence, but he'd set FBI agents to keep tabs on them all the same. What Hoover now learned from his own secret sources was that the Kennedys had been backed by Sam Giancana, and that Frank Sinatra was associated with the Chicago boss. It wasn't Sinatra he was out to get, of course, but the Kennedys.

The new president had tried in vain to oust Hoover from the F.B.I. Unable to do so, he appointed Bobby as attorney general, and that gave the Kennedys a power base within the FBI. Hoover was losing his grip on the Bureau, and he didn't like it. He had agents who were still loyal to him draw up a report that implicated Sinatra *and* the Kennedys with the Mafia. It could have been enough to bring down the presidency.

Meanwhile, Bobby got back to the job of investigating organised crime. The president was also looking for a way to break up the CIA because of their links to the Mafia, particularly following the government's bodged attempt to defeat Fidel Castro, the new Communist leader of Cuba. The CIA had hired Mafia hit men to try to assassinate Castro. They failed, and the question that has bothered many since is whether or not President Kennedy or his brother Bobby had ever sanctioned the use of Mafia assassins.

There was nothing new about the CIA's use of the Mafia. It stemmed from the Second World War, when the OSS, the Navy's own secret service, made a deal with Charles 'Lucky' Luciano to use mafiosi in Sicily and Italy to aid with the invasion of Sicily. When the Central Intelligence Agency was formed in 1947, it continued those links, through Johnny Roselli.

Frank Sinatra never got to like Johnny Roselli, who was responsible for the Mafia's 'sponsorship' of stars like George Raft, Gary Cooper, Jean Harlow, the Marx Brothers and Marilyn Monroe. There were, said Ava, some actors who would have found themselves in debt to the Mafia for the rest of their lives if it hadn't been for Frank Sinatra. He dissuaded a number of actors from accepting Roselli's help and, on occasions, gave a helping hand himself. Frank being Frank, he, like the Mafia, demanded that such people remember his favours. Unlike the Mafia, he wasn't likely to have them maimed or killed, but he did demand loyalty and respect, and when he didn't get it he cut those people off. That was the lesson Peter Lawford had learned.

Johnny Roselli complained to Giancana about Sinatra's interference, but Giancana simply told him that there were 'always plenty more fish in the sea'. Besides which, Giancana had more important work for Roselli. He gave him the task of strengthening the bond between the Mafia and the CIA. It is not known how many Mafia/CIA missions ever occurred, or how many Roselli was involved in, but he was an important part of the attempted invasion of Cuba at the Bay of Pigs in April 1961.

Sinatra knew this about Roselli. To Sinatra, a loyal American, it didn't matter if Mafia hit men were used to protect the freedom of every American. In fact, he firmly believed that the Mafia were exactly the right men for the job. He knew, too, about the CIA and how it had what some would describe as a 'Black Ops' force within it. He learned this from either Jack or Bobby Kennedy, who were both intent on bringing such operations to an end.

Peter Lawford was convinced the Kennedy brothers had only discovered the CIA/Mafia connection after Jack had come to office, and that the plan to kill Castro was already in the pipeline. Others dispute this. It is certainly true that the attempt by an American-backed force to invade Cuba at the Bay of Pigs, assisted by the Mafia, took place with the president's knowledge.

But, reasoned Lawford, even the president was unable to stop it going ahead. Lawford even thought that, for a while, Jack and Bobby had no great objections to the plan, if only so that they could be rid of a Communist leader in a neighbouring country. What Lawford was certain about is that, following the Bay of Pigs, the president had decided to break up the CIA, which, he realised had forces within it who were out of the government's control. Jack left the FBI to Bobby's control.

Giancana had always suspected that the Kennedys were not to be trusted and, faced with Bobby's determination to smash the Mafia, Mooney vowed to smash the presidency. There were agents at the FBI who had once been powerless to defeat organised crime because the Mafia had blackmailed Hoover, but they now backed Bobby to the hilt. The problem was that the CIA, or at least a faction within it, did not share the same aspirations as the FBI It was a tangled web into which Frank Sinatra was about to fall.

Chapter Nine

The Skinned Head of a Lamb

In 1961 the exiled Mafia boss Charles 'Lucky' Luciano decided to boost his ego with the idea of getting a film made about his life following his expulsion from America. He had his own biographer, Martin Gosch, write a 175-page screenplay that would show him in a sympathetic light. Luciano even had an actor in mind to portray him: Cary Grant. Gosch thought Grant an unlikely choice and suggested that a better actor would be Dean Martin. He, at least, was an Italian, he knew the kind of people who were of the same ilk as Luciano, and he had also had a very brief – though unsuccessful – career as a gangster himself in his early days.

Gosch didn't know Martin, so he had no idea how he would be able to get a copy of the script to him. For some reason, he decided it would be better to bypass Martin's agent and somehow place the screenplay directly in his hands.

Luciano said, 'Don't worry about that. I'll take care of it.'

Sammy Davis Jr knew about the proposed Lucky Luciano film because Dean Martin told him that Luciano had airmailed the screenplay to Sinatra, who passed it on. Martin told Davis, 'I didn't even read it. I resent the implication of being asked to play a character like that. Who do they think I am? George Raft?'

(Sammy thought Raft might actually have been a better choice, but since the death of his good pal Bugsy Siegel, the major studios had been less than keen on casting Raft in major roles.)

Davis said that Frank didn't even try to persuade Dean to do the film because he was of the same opinion. Sinatra said, 'It's bad enough that I got federal agents and reporters trying to tie me in with Luciano from way back, but if Dean played the part, they would all be jumping up and down and saying, "Look, Sinatra's pal is playing one of his other pals, so it's all gotta be true."'

So why did Sinatra pass the script to Martin in the first place? Because, said Davis, Luciano was an old friend and not one Frank wanted to offend. He was asked to do a simple favour, and he did it. He was under no obligation to take it any further.

Ever since Sinatra had been caught on camera by the FBI arriving in Havana in 1947 to visit Luciano, he'd been trying to quell the story. And so Davis was surprised that Sinatra had even agreed to do as much for Luciano as passing on the script to Dean Martin, because the last thing Frank needed was someone making yet another link between him and Lucky Luciano.

Luciano even tried to help Sinatra by stating, 'I don't wanna give the idea that he was ever asked to do somethin' illegal, by me or by anybody else that I know of. He gave out a few presents to different guys, like a gold cigarette case, a watch, that kind of thing, but that was it. As for me, the guy was always number-one okay.'

That did not help Sinatra much. Over the years he found himself constantly repeating his claim that he had only been in Havana for a holiday and just happened to find himself having dinner with a group of men and women he didn't know – and that when he discovered that one of the men was Lucky Luciano, he was surprised. 'It suddenly struck me that I was laying myself open to criticism by remaining at the table,' he went on record as saying. 'But I could think of no way to leave the table without creating a scene.' He admitted to running into Luciano at the Hotel Nacional's casino, 'where I had a quick drink, and excused myself. Those were the only times I have ever seen Luciano in my life.'

I asked Sammy Davis if Sinatra really did know Lucky Luciano. He replied, 'Why else would a guy like Lucky Luciano send Frank Sinatra a script, saying, "Please pass this on to Dean Martin"?'

The beginning of the end of the Rat Pack – or the Summit – was said to have started during a comeback by Eddie Fisher. He was then married to Elizabeth Taylor and had become better known as being Liz Taylor's husband rather than an entertainer in his own right. Liz had been filming *Cleopatra* in England for three months when the picture was suddenly closed down due to an illness that nearly killed Liz, a change in director and a change in location. New sets were being constructed in Italy.

Fisher was finding it a long stretch between his own professional engagements while he waited for Liz to make *Cleopatra*. It had been eighteen months since he had last performed, so in May 1961, he returned to the stage to perform at the Desert Inn in Las Vegas. Then he played the Coconut Grove in Los Angeles, and virtually the whole of Hollywood society turned up at the opening night, including the Summit. As soon as Fisher walked on, Sinatra and his cronies, all of them drunk, began heckling him and ended up climbing onto the stage to take over the show.

Fisher simply took a seat and sat there while the Summit went into one of their Sands routines. The audience began booing them, bringing the act to a speedy conclusion, and when they finally left the stage Fisher got up and said to the audience, 'Join me in singing "God Bless America" to show President Kennedy we're behind him.' That won back the audience. But, as Fisher noted, 'My opening night at the Coconut Grove was the beginning of the end of the Rat Pack.' If it was the beginning of the end, then it was a long, slow decline. To Fisher, perhaps, it was an indication that the Rat Pack's popularity and power had just peaked.

There was still some mileage to be had in the old pack, however. Later in 1961 the Summit were summoned for another movie, *Sergeants Three*, a western remake of *Gunga Din*. It would be the last time that Peter Lawford would make a film with Frank, Sammy, Dean and Joey.

Sinatra followed this film with a non-Summit picture which would not have been made at all, had it not been for the friendship between Frank and the president. The picture was *The Manchurian Candidate*, directed by John Frankenheimer. Frank was to play a Korean War veteran who becomes puzzled by the behaviour of an ex-comrade, who turns out to have been brainwashed by the North Koreans into turning traitor. Richard Condon, who wrote the book, had based it on a story he had heard which was purported to be true.

Like Stanley Kramer, Frankenheimer had reservations about working with Frank Sinatra. Yet he found in him an ally who was instrumental in getting the film made through his connections to the White House when United Artists president Arthur Krim refused to back the film. Frankenheimer and the screenwriter George Axelrod had managed to acquire the screen rights to the book, plus a commitment from Sinatra even before a screenplay was produced. Frankenheimer told me:

'If it had not been for Frank Sinatra's friendship with President Kennedy, the film would not have been made. George Axelrod and myself went to see Arthur Krim at United Artists with a proposal to do the film, and Krim said, "I won't make this picture. Not only will I not make it, but I'll call every studio in town and tell them they shouldn't make it. I won't have that book made into a movie."

'I said, "But why not?"

'He said, "Do you think we're going to embarrass our president by putting all this in a picture? You've got to be out of your mind."

'The problem with Krim was simply that he was a Democrat – he even later became finance chairman to the Democratic Party – and he saw the book, and of course, the film we wanted to make, as a criticism of what we sent our soldiers to do and what happened to some of them.

'George flew out to California to meet with Frank and told him what Krim had said. Frank said, "Leave it to me," and he personally called President Kennedy and told him the problem.

'The president told Sinatra he had read the book and had no objection to it. He told Frank, "This film should be made. I want you to make it. I'd consider it a personal favour if you made it."

'Frank asked the president, "Since Arthur Krim is a friend of yours, would you call him and tell him this?"

'And the president did call Krim, and told him to make the picture.'

Laurence Harvey, who played the brainwashed veteran, had heard all the horror stories about Sinatra's volatile behaviour and Mob-style antics. He expected some fireworks on the set from his co-star, but he wasn't prepared for Sinatra's own personal and rather dubious way of making friends. Harvey became extremely alarmed when he was given the typescript of an article for a magazine in which Sinatra said that Harvey was a Communist and that he had a habit of kissing men in public. He sent his press agent to see Frank, to ask why he had said those things. Sinatra told him, 'I knew that Larry had approval of the article, so I said those things as a gag. That's all. It'll never get into print. It was just a practical joke.'

It may have been an odd way for anyone to show friendship, but fortunately Harvey took it in good humour, showing that he was on the same wavelength as Frank, and they got on well. Sinatra, in his own way, was mellowing – but there would still be times in the future when he would use his own Mob-style tactics to prove a point.

The Manchurian Candidate was a tight, taut thriller with a clear message – Communism was bad for your health. The fact that Frank made the film virtually as a favour to John F Kennedy was evidence of the esteem in which the president then held Sinatra. Frank enjoyed the laurels that came with being the president's friend – probably more than the rewards that came with being a friend to the boss of the Chicago Outfit.

That boss, Sam Giancana, knew he was in a tight spot because Bobby Kennedy was intent on exposing him and all his associates in organised crime. In an effort to stop events before they went too far, Sam met with Sinatra at a hotel in Florida and asked for his help to influence the Kennedys.

Frank told him, 'Don't worry about it. I'm gonna talk to the president.'

Some time later, Giancana met with Sinatra again and asked why Bobby was still investigating the Mob. Sinatra told him, 'It's okay. I talked to Bobby.'

The truth was, Sinatra wasn't saying anything about Giancana to any of the Kennedys. He continued to make vague promises to Giancana about talking to old Joe Kennedy, but he didn't want to antagonise the president or any of his family. He valued his friendship with them all, but all he succeeded in doing was to antagonise the Mob, Giancana especially.

Giancana sent Johnny Roselli to tell Sinatra to talk to the Kennedys, to try to get Bobby to back off.

Frank told Roselli, 'Johnny, I took Sam's name, and wrote it down, and told Bobby Kennedy: "This is my buddy, this is what I want you to know, Bob."'

He also told Roselli that he had spoken to Joe Kennedy three times. That wasn't true. Frank was saying nothing to Joe or any other Kennedy to try to protect Giancana.

Sam the Cigar lost patience with Frank and told Johnny Roselli, 'One minute Frank says he's talked to Robert, and the next minute he says he hasn't talked to him. So, he never did talk to him. It's a lot of shit. Why lie to me? I haven't got that coming. When he says he's gonna do a guy a little favour, I don't give a shit how long it takes. He's got to give you a little favour.'

It was suggested to Giancana that it was time to teach Sinatra a lesson in respect, and Mooney agreed. He decided to send Sinatra a message in no uncertain terms. The film director Melville Shavelson recalled the incident:

'Paramount had sent me to see Frank Sinatra with a script, *Easter Dinner* – which we later did as *The Pigeon who Took Rome* with Charlton Heston. I went up to his penthouse suite and there were these guys sitting outside. I said, "I've come to see Frank with a script."

'They said, "You're not going in there."

'I said, "Why not?"

'They said, "Nobody goes in."

'I said, "But I'm here to show Frank this script."

'And they said, "Doesn't matter. He's not seeing anyone."

'I said, "Why not, guys?"

'They said, "Mr Sinatra ordered room service, and when it arrived he took the cover off the silver plate, and instead of his dinner, there was the skinned head of a lamb." That was the Mafia code for death.'

Sinatra, shaken by this, hid himself away for several days, with bodyguards to keep everyone – and that meant *everyone* – out, including important film directors. If the Mafia could somehow replace the dinner he'd ordered with the skinned head of a lamb, they were perfectly capable of getting anyone they liked into his penthouse.

When Sinatra later told Ava about this, she asked him, 'Didn't that make you realise how deep you'd got yourself in with those hoods?'

He replied, 'Nah! After a few days, I realised it was all a bluff, and I just got on with my life.'

Ava felt that Sinatra's attitude was itself a bluff, and he did challenge Giancana directly about the lamb's head. Giancana denied that it had come from him. Frank knew better. By this time he had learned a great deal about how the Mafia operated, and although he didn't hire gangsters himself, he did have his own bodyguards, who would sort out any little problems with anyone who caused him trouble. It would be too much of a cliché to call this group of men Sinatra's Mafia (as, for instance, Howard Hughes's bodyguards were known as the Mormon Mafia), and such a description would be unfair and untrue since they did not carry out the kind of nefarious activities associated with the Mafia. Nonetheless, Sinatra had modelled his own little mob on the Mafia, and they were the kind of men who were able to gain information. Ava was sure that some of them were private detectives, and they were able to report to Sinatra that Giancana had, indeed, ordered the death threat.

It would take a second message of death, a year later, to make Sinatra realise he that wasn't as untouchable as he'd thought.

An indication that Sinatra had mellowed came from an interview I did with Rex Harrison, who admitted that he had treated Sinatra with such disrespect 'it's a wonder he didn't have my legs broken'. He said:

'I first met Frank around 1945 when I was in Hollywood with Lilly [Palmer], who was then my wife, and John and Mary Mills. I can't remember how we first met exactly, but Frank invited all of us to stay at his home. It was very cordial. I think Sinatra liked English actors. But he struck me as being a bit of a "hood", as the Americans say.

'When I finished doing *My Fair Lady* on Broadway [in 1961], I was then engaged to Kay [Kendall], who was making a film in Hollywood called *Les Girls*. Well, when you're in Hollywood you get invited to the most lavish parties, which I really quite enjoyed, and one of the parties was at the home of producer Charles Feldman.

'Frank Sinatra was there, and I got awfully jealous of the attention he was paying to Kay. After a while she disappeared, and I couldn't see Sinatra anywhere either. I found them together on the patio, and Kay insisted she was just admiring Frank's shirt. "What a beautiful shirt this is, don't you agree?" she said to me.

'Well, I had heard about his reputation with the women and was positive he was flirting with Kay, and so I looked him in the eye and said, "What colour is it?"

'He replied, "What colour is what?"

'I said through my teeth – which hurt because I was gritting them so hard – "The shirt!"

'By now we were locked together in a minor battle of will. He said, "I guess you could call it a sort of yellow."

'Well, I knew he wasn't talking about the shirt, so I slapped him round the face. He just stood there, and I noticed his fists were clenched and just knew we were in for a fistfight. But he didn't hit me. He just said, "It's still yellow."

'So I slapped him again. He just turned and walked away. Only later did Terence Rattigan, who was at the party, point out to me that no one could insult Frank Sinatra and get away with it – but I did, only because he knew he could have flattened me with one punch and, for some reason, decided not to. I have no idea why. I was told he was later laughing about the incident.

'But I was still green with jealousy and left the party, and just went walking around Beverly Hills, convinced Kay didn't love me. All very petty. Terence Rattigan came looking for me with Kay, and told me not to be a baby, and he took us both off for a weekend in Palm Springs to stay with Bing Crosby, who was a very nice gentleman indeed. Crosby was also clever. He called Sinatra and asked him to come over, and we shook hands. He told me, "You could have gone on hitting me all night and I wouldn't have hit you back because I admire you." That takes a big man – a bigger man than me. But I wouldn't say we parted company the best of friends.

'Still, you had to admire the man as an entertainer. I remember when I was ill in 1969, I was feeling very sorry for myself and was watching Sinatra on television. I felt compelled to write him a letter to let him know how much pleasure his performance had given me and how it lifted my spirits. He kindly wrote back and said he hoped we would meet some time in the future.

'A few years later we happened to meet him in London in Claridges. [Harrison was then married to Elizabeth Harris]. He was performing in London and invited us to see the show as his personal guests.'

This was a vastly different Sinatra from the one who pushed his weight around in the fifties. If Rex Harrison had offended him then, Sinatra would undoubtedly never have spoken to him again.

Chapter Ten

Weekend at the Cal-Neva

Frank heard that the president wanted to spend some time away from politics, somewhere close to Hollywood, while his wife was away in India and Pakistan, and so he invited 'the Prez' to come and stay at his Palm Springs home in March 1962. The president accepted.

Johnny Roselli reported all this to Giancana, to illustrate that Sinatra was showing full respect to the Kennedys and none at all to Sam. Again it was suggested that a contract be put on Sinatra. Giancana told Roselli there would be no contract, arguing that they couldn't just kill the most famous entertainer in the world – this despite the fact that he had already threatened Sinatra with death. Ava said that Giancana's reason for not touching Frank was just an excuse because he needed him for other business ventures he had in mind – 'otherwise he would have had Frank killed for sure'.

To accommodate the president, Sinatra made some extensive improvements to his Palm Springs home, including the building of a heliport just so the president could land there. Unfortunately, he failed to get a permit to have helicopters land there, and the heliport became a white elephant.

Meanwhile, Hoover had been keeping busy compiling reports on Sinatra, Giancana and the Kennedys. One report claimed that one of Sam Giancana's girlfriends, Judith Campbell Exner, was also a mistress of Jack Kennedy. The wire taps at the Cal-Neva Lodge had proved most useful to Hoover.

Hoover came to the conclusion, erroneously, that Sinatra was the man responsible for introducing Giancana to Kennedy. It may be that Hoover knew all about Joe Kennedy's behind-the-scenes activities to use the Mafia to get Jack into the White House, but it was Jack and Bobby for whom Hoover was really gunning. And he knew he had something of a smoking gun to use against the Kennedys – Frank Sinatra. According to Ava, 'Frank, like Lee Harvey Oswald, was a patsy.'

The official version of what happened next was that Bobby Kennedy had a report drawn up from FBI files, probably in February 1962, regarding Sinatra's associations with the Mafia. It read:

> Sinatra has had a long and wide association with hoodlums and racketeers which seems to be continuing. The nature of Sinatra's work may, on occasion, bring him into contact with underworld figures, but this cannot account for his friendship and/or financial involvement with people such as Joe and Rocco Fischetti, cousins of Al Capone, Paul Emilio D'Amato, John Formosa and Sam Giancana, all of whom are on our list of racketeers. No other entertainer appears to be mentioned nearly so often with racketeers.
>
> Available information indicates not only that Sinatra is associated with each of the above-mentioned racketeers but that they apparently maintain contact with one another. This indicates a possible community of interest involving Sinatra and racketeers in Illinois, Indiana, New Jersey, Florida and Nevada.

According to the official version, which has gone down as

history, Bobby recommended to brother Jack that, because of this report, he should not stay at Sinatra's home. Bobby told Peter Lawford to break the news to Frank, who, upon hearing the ill tidings, went into a rage and thereafter never spoke to Lawford again. Thus runs the official account, which Peter Lawford perpetuated.

In a formal interview I had with Lawford in 1974, he told me, 'Frank always blamed Pat and me for the break-up of his friendship with the president, which was preposterous because we had nothing to do with it, but he saw it as an act of betrayal. What betrayed Frank was his own friendship with Sam Giancana and that was enough to bring his association with the president to an end. Frank never spoke to me again.'

It was also said that Sinatra blamed Bobby Kennedy for the president cancelling his stay at his home, and got him on the phone, calling him, as Peter Lawford put it, 'every name under the sun'.

In another private meeting, and at the insistence of Ava Gardner, Lawford told me the truth about his eventual falling-out with Sinatra. However, the implications of that particular truth would have been devastating in the light of what was to happen (which will become clear in due course), and so for years Lawford maintained the 'official' story to protect himself, the Kennedys and – unwillingly – Sinatra.

As Ava and Sammy Davis both noted, the official version was 'all crap'. Bobby and Jack were fully aware of Sinatra's friendship and business association with Giancana long before all this, so it could not have come as any surprise to Bobby to discover the FBI files naming Sinatra in connection with racketeers. 'They all goddamn knew,' said Ava, 'so it was no great shock to the president or to the attorney general.'

In fact, just a few months earlier, Jack and Bobby had been at a party at Lawford's Santa Monica beach house, where, among the guests, were Sinatra and Marilyn Monroe. In my formal interview with Peter Lawford, he said that Bobby took Sinatra aside and told him that his links with Giancana could become an embarrassment to the president and that, if he wanted to maintain his friendship, he would have to break away from Giancana. Sinatra, in his own belligerent way, told Bobby that nobody told him what to do.

In a later interview at Ava's home, however, Lawford admitted to me that, while Bobby did mention that they all needed to be careful, there was no 'it's either Giancana or us' threat. They had all been 'in bed together over the presidential campaign', they had all been to the Cal-Neva Lodge, they had all taken advantage of the set-up Giancana had arranged so that the Kennedy brothers could have any girls they wanted in the privacy of their own bungalow. Sinatra had never known that the bungalow had been bugged, and had no idea what Giancana's intentions were. He would later find out what Mooney had been up to, and promised he would get his revenge – for that and other things.

The FBI report, as far as I can gather, was actually drawn up in August 1962 and not February, long after this event brought about the parting of the ways between JFK and Frank Sinatra. Regardless of the date of the report, however, Bobby Kennedy did not volunteer the details to his brother willingly. It was Hoover who virtually forced the report upon Bobby, and it was all part of Hoover's plan to undermine the Kennedys. He was showing them that he had plenty of dirt on them if he chose to use it.

Bobby, afraid that Hoover would find an excuse to bury them with the report, talked to Jack, but they both agreed they should not let Hoover push them into a corner now, or they would be forever at his mercy.

In the end it was decided that the president should not stay at Sinatra's home following a report Bobby had received from his most trusted security agents: there were too many security risks, and Bing Crosby's home was deemed be a safer bet. However, while this story seems to have been confirmed by Nancy Sinatra for one, Ava maintained that the Kennedys reluctantly agreed that they both needed to keep their distance from Sinatra – if only for a while, until they could get Hoover out of the picture altogether.

It is true that Peter and Pat Lawford were given the task of delivering the message, but Sinatra did not shoot the messengers. He did fly into a drunken rage about it, but he did not blame Lawford. He tried to get Bobby on the phone, but the attorney general avoided taking the call, which means that Sinatra did not, after all, call Bobby 'every name under the sun' over the phone – although he did to those within earshot.

As Davis recalled, 'It was a pure slap in the face, as far as Frank was concerned. He'd really helped Kennedy get to the White House, and it had nothing to do with what Mooney had been up to.' But, said Davis, the president was in a difficult situation, and Frank knew it. As it turned out, according to Davis, the president called Sinatra from Crosby's house and they talked things over. 'Frank understood,' said Davis, 'but he didn't like it.'

To show there were no hard feelings – even if there were many – Frank sent the president a rocking chair for his birthday that year. Not only that, but Kennedy personally urged Sinatra to make the film *The Manchurian Candidate*. The friendship was still there, but it was being maintained in a low-key manner. It is possible that the friendship between the president and Sinatra might have returned to normal in due course, but another, far more tragic, event was to seal the fate of that relationship.

Giancana was delighted when he got the news that the president had jilted Sinatra. There was a strange and strained friendship between Frank and Mooney by that time. Frank had become wary of Giancana since receiving his death threat, even though Giancana assured him that it had not come from him. By and large, however, Sinatra still felt safe enough because he knew that Giancana needed him.

It must have come as a kind of bonus to Giancana to discover that after JFK had finished with Marilyn Monroe, whom he had been meeting for a series of sexual liaisons, his brother Bobby moved in on her. Not only did Giancana have wires at Lawford's house, but also at the Cal-Neva, and at Monroe's home. It was at her Beverly Hills bungalow that she and Bobby often met.

Despite all the opinions to the contrary, Lawford maintained that there was an affair going on between Bobby and Marilyn. Why did Lawford allow himself to become the go-between in the first place? It was simply because he did not have the strength of Sinatra, who was prepared to say no every now and then, even to the likes of Giancana. When the Kennedys asked Lawford to do something for them, being their brother-in-law, he did it. He was never proud of that fact, and would come to regret all he had done.

Ava thought that Frank and Marilyn rekindled their affair in 1961 – and this time it was a lot more intense. It was one of the few affairs Frank had that the public knew nothing about. It would seem that Monroe led something of a fantasy existence, possibly due to her drug dependency. She had the idea that Frank wanted to marry her, but Sinatra had publicly said that he would never marry another woman whose career was show business. (This, however, did not stop him later announcing that he would marry the actress/singer/dancer Juliet Prowse, and even later actually marrying Mia Farrow.) Early on in their affair, Sinatra definitely did not want to marry Monroe. He liked what they had between them and did not want to spoil it. He would later change his mind.

In August 1961, Sinatra arranged for a party on board his yacht just for himself and Marilyn, and Dean and Jeanne Martin. Marilyn was at Sinatra's house before they embarked on their sailing trip, and Frank was getting impatient waiting for her. He finally asked Jeanne, 'Will you please go and get Marilyn dressed so we can get in the limo and go?'

Jeanne Martin said, 'She couldn't get herself organised, but she was the one person Frank was patient with.'

Their affair seems to have come to an end by the beginning of 1962, when Frank had become emotionally drained trying to help a woman he saw as someone who only wanted to kill herself. He didn't wash his hands of her altogether, though. He would be there when she needed him.

The episode regarding Marilyn Monroe's presence at the Cal-Neva during the last weekend of July 1962, just a week before her death, is surrounded in contradictions. This is the way it was told to me.

Bobby Kennedy had decided to end his affair with Marilyn and was looking forward to a weekend in Los Angeles. He asked – or rather told – Peter Lawford to get Marilyn out of Los Angeles for the weekend and also to be the messenger of bad tidings: Peter had the job of telling Marilyn that Bobby had dumped her.

Marilyn's love life was already in turmoil, mainly because of her weakness when it came to dealing with the facts of her own life. She was of the naive opinion that Bobby was going to divorce his wife and marry her. She was also still carrying a torch for Joe DiMaggio. On top of that, Frank Sinatra had come to the conclusion that he wanted to marry her after all, partly because he was still in love with her – although she was clearly not as in love with him as he was with her – and partly because he felt that he had a better chance than anyone of protecting her from her own self-destructive personality.

There are claims that Sinatra invited her to Cal-Neva for that weekend as a favour to Bobby Kennedy. Ava and Lawford both rubbished that notion. Although Frank still had aspirations to rebuild his friendship with the president, he had developed a certain contempt for Bobby – perhaps because Bobby was the one leading the campaign to smash organised crime, which, in turn, posed a threat to Frank because of his associations. Nevertheless, Sinatra had assurances from the Kennedys that he would not be implicated. They were only after the big guns, like Sam Giancana.

The conundrum for Sinatra was that Giancana was still his friend and secret business associate, while at the same time there had been a growing antipathy between Sinatra and Giancana. A death threat from your so-called friend is hardly a solid foundation on which to maintain a friendship. On the one hand Sinatra was trying to set aside his past troubles with Giancana, and on the other he was wary of the consequences of such a friendship, as well he should have been when dealing with a cold-blooded murderer. Then again, Sinatra was no saint. He tended to judge his Mafia friends with more tolerance than the average citizen because he understood the nature of their business. Nonetheless, he had not completely forgiven Giancana for sending him the skinned head of that lamb.

There was also the simple matter of business. Much of Sinatra's money was tied up in Mafia-run businesses, notably the Sands and the Cal-Neva. Regardless of any assurances from the Kennedy fold, as delivered by Peter Lawford, he still stood to lose much by Bobby's anti-Mafia campaign.

So Frank was not inclined to do Bobby a favour by inviting Marilyn to the Cal-Neva. Peter Lawford, however, imposed upon Sinatra to allow him and Pat to bring Marilyn to the lodge for that weekend. Sinatra agreed because, more than anything, he wanted to keep an eye on Marilyn himself, fearful of that self-destructive force within her. It was also a favour to Peter Lawford, a man who was still his friend, despite the reports to the contrary.

Sinatra sent his private plane, *Christina*, to collect Marilyn as well as Peter and Pat Lawford. Had Sinatra hated Lawford at that time, he would surely not have allowed him to set foot on his private plane. Also, the fact that Lawford was allowed entry into the Cal-Neva was proof enough that he and Sinatra were still friends. Some have said that the only reason Sinatra allowed Lawford into the Cal-Neva that weekend was for the sake of Marilyn. Ava made it clear that, had Sinatra really held a grudge against Lawford, he would have thrown him off the premises himself and maintained his own vigilance on Marilyn. As it was, Lawford and Sinatra agreed that the best thing for Marilyn was for them both to keep an eye on her. As it would prove, however, two sets of eyes were not enough.

Peter and Pat Lawford duly told Marilyn that Frank had invited them all to the Cal-Neva for the weekend, and Monroe was only too delighted to go. What they hadn't reckoned on was that Marilyn told Johnny Roselli that she would be at the Lodge that weekend – and Roselli told Sam Giancana. Giancana made a point of being there too. Ever since he had seen Monroe's *Playboy* calendar photo, he'd wanted to sleep with her.

Whether or not Marilyn had previously met Giancana, no one who spoke to me said – probably because they didn't know. She certainly knew who he was: Johnny had often spoken to her about how Mr Giancana had been the power behind her initial introduction to stardom. She was not shy of the Mafia. The FBI had eyeballed her with certain known mobsters in Hollywood, so she was far from ignorant about the Mafia. In fact, having had an affair with Sinatra, which now seemed on the point of being rekindled, she could not help but know about them. She certainly knew the truth about Johnny Roselli's real purpose in Hollywood. Ava was sure that Frank himself would have reassured her at some point that these men were his friends and she should not fear them: he would always protect her from harm.

Marilyn also knew about Giancana because of her affair with Bobby Kennedy. Lawford said that Bobby had been careless in telling her too much – about the CIA/Mafia operations, about Bobby's own determination to break the Mafia, and how Sinatra was an associate of Giancana. That was another reason why Sinatra had no great fondness for Bobby.

The exact sequence of events at the Cal-Neva is hard to pin down because there are so many contradictory reports, but what follows is the order of events as I recall it being told to me.

Frank was performing, so he had little opportunity to maintain a constant vigilance on Marilyn. While he sang, Peter Lawford stayed with her. Then came the blow: Lawford finally told Marilyn that her affair with Bobby was over. She became extremely distraught at the news. She had drunk a lot – they all had – and she began to lose control.

Frank saw what was happening and at the first chance he had, he and Lawford took Marilyn outside in an effort to calm her down. There are stories of how she was not only drunk but also drugged, but Lawford disputed this. She didn't need drugs to make her veer emotionally out of control, and certainly the alcohol she'd consumed didn't help to stabilise her.

She swore that she was going to 'go public' on her affair with the Kennedys, and said she would call a press conference to tell the world how she had been used. She swore that she'd reveal everything Bobby had told her – much to Sinatra's alarm, who figured that she meant she'd blow the lid off the whole CIA/Mafia set-up, not to mention how Jack had been aided in his presidential campaign by the Mafia.

It seems that they did manage to calm her down – without having to resort to drugging her – and, once back inside, she sat down while Frank returned to the stage to continue the show. That was about the time Sam Giancana joined the not-so-happy party at their table.

Oozing all the charm he could muster – which, according to Lawford, was not much – Giancana told Marilyn that he could see she was upset, and he asked her to tell him all about it. She obviously felt comfortable in his presence, based on Johnny Roselli's glowing reports about her 'sponsor', and so she did tell him everything. Lawford said she was so drunk she hardly knew what she was saying, and he kept trying politely to shut her up. In the event, she told Giancana all about the press conference she was going to call. Giancana smiled and told her she shouldn't worry herself about 'that rat Bobby', and he quickly managed to win her confidence. Even a naive, weak woman like Monroe might have known better than to tell Giancana about her intentions, but she was very drunk, and with him lending a sympathetic ear, she was singing like the proverbial canary. And, like a canary, she was trapped in Sam's cage.

Frank saw them in conversation, and when he had the chance to speak to Giancana alone, he asked what had gone on. Sam told him.

Frank said, 'She doesn't know what she's saying. Let me handle her.'

'You worry too much, Frank.'

'What's to worry about?'

'Nothing at all. Leave it to me. I'll see to it that our little problem sitting over there goes away.'

'Marilyn isn't the problem. Bobby Kennedy's the problem.'

'That's what I mean. I got everything under control.'

Sinatra didn't like the sound of that at all. He tried to assure himself that Sam would probably take care of Marilyn in the nicest sense, but deep down he had a nagging doubt about it all.

Giancana returned to the table and suggested to Marilyn that she go with him to his bungalow, where they could talk over her problems about Bobby. He'd fix things for her, he said.

When Lawford told Sinatra that Monroe had gone with Sam, Frank yelled at him, 'What the fuck did you let her go with him for?'

'What am I going to do? Tell Sam Giancana to mind his own business?'

There is a story that, somehow, Marilyn managed to get a call through to Joe DiMaggio to come and get her. He apparently turned up later at the Cal-Neva, but was denied access. None of this was related to me, and so I can't even begin to make an assumption as to how true it is. If it did happen, it conjures up a somewhat poignant picture of Joe standing outside the grounds, hopeless and helpless to rescue Marilyn, who was to spend the night in Sam Giancana's bungalow.

The next morning Giancana handed a roll of film to Sinatra, saying he'd taken pictures of Marilyn that night and wanted to have the film developed. Frank gave the roll of film to a trusted employee, and when the employee returned with the developed photos, Frank was sickened by what he saw. There was Monroe, in the nude, on the floor of Sam's bungalow, totally drunk and by then probably drugged, obviously in no control of herself. The photos were pure pornography.

Frank asked his employee, 'Have you seen these?'

'Yeah.'

'Not very nice, are they?'

'No.'

'Get rid of them.'

The employee destroyed the photos and the negatives. When Giancana asked for his pictures, Sinatra told him that they had not come out. Sam joked that he was obviously a lousy photographer, but Sinatra sensed that Giancana knew he was lying and he seemed pleased to think that Frank had seen the pictures and been so disgusted.

It has been said that it was Sinatra himself who took the photos. Another version has both Frank and Giancana in the bungalow with Marilyn, taking the photos. Yet both Ava, who only had Frank's version of events, and Lawford, who knew very well that Marilyn had spent the entire night with Giancana, said that it was Sam who'd taken the pictures himself. My impression is that the version Ava and Lawford gave is the correct one because, if nothing else, Sinatra was so fond of Marilyn, that it is inconceivable that he would have treated her in such a disgusting and demeaning way. For Giancana to have treated her thus – that's a different matter.

Chapter Eleven

A Murder Conspiracy Uncovered

A week later, on Sunday 5 August, Marilyn's nude body was found in circumstances so contradictory that the truth of what really happened has been a never-ending quest for the most ardent authors.

Officially, she killed herself by swallowing as many as fifty Nembutal sleeping tablets in a matter of seconds, and her body was discovered at some point early on Sunday morning (times vary and have never been confirmed) by her housekeeper, Mrs Eunice Murray, and her psychiatrist, Dr Ralph Greenson. An incomplete autopsy was carried out, and no inquest was held.

There has been so much information and disinformation about the events surrounding her death that it has remained a constant source of fascination for writers and television producers ever since, with countless books and documentaries on the subject. Very few of them have come close to the truth. The few who have come close have just missed it by a mark.

Those who did get to the truth were Frank Sinatra and Peter Lawford, and for reasons of their own, neither was ever going to go public with it. In fact, as far as Peter Lawford was concerned, he would, over time, create a sensational myth regarding Monroe's so-called suicide. In 1962 he said that he had called Marilyn by phone on the Saturday evening at seven o'clock, because she was expected over for dinner and had not arrived. She had said she wouldn't be over because she was sleepy and had a busy Sunday ahead of her. 'She said she felt happy and was going to bed,' was his story in 1962. Over the years that story evolved into something more. In a formal interview with me in 1974, he told me: I'd been expecting Marilyn to show up around eight, and when she didn't I called her and said, 'What happened to you?'

Her voice was weird, sleepy, fuzzy. She said she wasn't going to make it. She was too tired. She'd had a quarrel with Pat Newcomb and Pat had gone home. Then she said, 'Say goodbye to Pat, say goodbye to the president, and say goodbye to yourself because you're a nice guy.'

When somebody says goodbye, I figure that's terminal. I felt I had to get over to her bungalow and check on her but my manager [Milt Ebbins] said, 'You can't go over there. You're the brother-in-law of the president of the United States. Your wife's away. Let me get in touch with her doctor or lawyer. They can help her.'

I said, 'But she said goodbye to me. She may be dying.' It was too late. There is nothing worse in life than being unable to turn back the clock. If I could do that, maybe Marilyn would be alive today.

The story he was to give me just weeks later at Ava's house, under the influence of a great deal of alcohol, probably some drugs, and at the insistence of Ava, was very different. This was the version of events he had previously told Ava, and in order to prevent the facts from being lost in a haze of drink – or drug-induced mumbling, she prompted and guided him. He also told a different story to one of his later wives, Deborah Gould, in which he admitted his part in a cover-up (I shall explain this later on), but maintained that Marilyn had committed suicide. He said to Deborah that he told Marilyn,

'For God's sake, don't leave any notes behind.' According to Deborah, he said he did find a suicide note and had destroyed it. Yet that, as shall be seen, was not the case.

One of the first people Frank spoke to upon hearing the news of Marilyn's death was Sam Giancana, who told him, 'I said we'd sort out our little problem.'

'What the fuck does that mean?' demanded Sinatra.

'It means that our boy Bobby is in the fucking hot seat.'

Sinatra wasn't convinced that was all Giancana meant. Then he called Ava in Spain.

The next thing he did was to call a meeting of the Summit – or at least the majority of it. Sammy Davis was most revealing about this particular event. He, Lawford and Dean Martin were present. Joey Bishop was not mentioned.

They were all stunned by the tragic news. Dean in particular was distraught because he had been working with Marilyn over at 20th Century Fox in *Something's Gotta Give*. It was widely known that Marilyn had been fired from the film because of her persistent absence from the set. During filming her behaviour had become increasingly erratic, and on one occasion there was an attempt by Marilyn to reach Sinatra by phone from the studio, only to find he was on a world tour.

George Cukor, renowned for his reputation as a director who was at his best with actresses, was at the helm of *Something's Gotta Give*, but he was totally unable to hit the mark with Monroe. After one particular scene in which she failed to deliver a line through ten takes, Cukor yelled at her, sending her fleeing to her dressing room in tears. On her mirror she scrawled with a red lipstick, 'Frank, help me. Frank, please help me.'

After she was fired, there was much talk about replacing her, but Dean Martin had insisted that either Marilyn did the film, or he'd walk. Just a few days before her death, Marilyn had been told she was back in the film.

Apparently, Sinatra had also been involved in negotiations with Fox about the situation when he found out that Marilyn had been fired. There was no suggestion of any heavy-handed tactics of the Mafia kind. Instead, Sinatra had virtually given a personal guarantee that she would turn up every day for work, although he couldn't guarantee that she would be on time. That was the bug every producer had to bear when casting Monroe. She would arrive for filming when she was ready. Sinatra had the same attitude. He was a star, and it was a sign of his own arrogance that he could turn up for work when he was ready. He certainly wasn't going to force Marilyn to do any different. But, he said, she would be on set every day.

In effect, between them, Martin and Sinatra had prevented Monroe's career from coming to a premature end – or so they thought. The fact that, following her death, the newspapers were filled with stories of how depressed she had been, particularly because of being fired from the film, told them that something was not right. Since getting the news that she was going back to work, she had been anything but depressed.

Obviously, she still felt betrayed by Bobby Kennedy and that was a source of some pain. But Marilyn had lived a complicated love life, and Sinatra was not convinced that this alone was enough to drive her to suicide. In fact, he had finally told her that he wanted to marry her – although she had apparently not given him an answer. All he wanted to do was protect her. (Sammy Davis felt that Sinatra would have gone ahead with the wedding had she lived. He doubted, however, that the marriage would have had much of a chance because eventually Frank would have grown tired – as he already had done previously – of trying to keep her stable and happy.)

It was at that private meeting of the Summit that Peter Lawford admitted his part in the events prior to and following Marilyn's death, and of his participation in a massive cover-up.

He explained how Bobby Kennedy had been at his house during Saturday 4 August. In fact, Bobby had been over to see Marilyn in the afternoon to try to make her see reason. She had become hysterical, and an injection had been administered to sedate her – either by Bobby's own physician or by Marilyn's: there is still speculation regarding that fact. An injection was given nonetheless, and Bobby left to return to Lawford's house.

Lawford, concerned for Marilyn, had called her and invited her over to his house that evening. There may have been a few more phone calls from Lawford's house to Marilyn's, but there was certainly no desperate call from a sleepy Marilyn telling Lawford to 'say goodbye to the president'. That was Lawford's own invention.

Sometime later in the evening, Lawford got a call to say that Marilyn had been found unconscious, and he rushed to her home, accompanied by some of Bobby's secret service agents. They called for an ambulance, and she was whisked away.

A little while later her dead body was returned. As Lawford put it to me, he was beside himself and not thinking straight. He called Bobby with the news and was ordered to make sure that he and the agents 'cleaned up' the scene. Lawford also had to arrange for a helicopter to fly Bobby out of Los Angeles. Bobby would deny he had ever been in town that day.

Lawford at first wondered if Bobby had been responsible in some way for Marilyn's death. He said he was on 'autopilot' as he simply did as he was told. A number of people present at Marilyn's bungalow needed to be involved in what proved to be a conspiracy to protect Bobby's secret affair with Monroe. There was the housekeeper Mrs Eunice Murray, Marilyn's psychiatrist Dr Greenson, her physician Dr Engelberg, and others, including publicist Arthur P Jacobs.

In 1970 I met Jacobs, who told me that he had been at the Hollywood Bowl that Saturday evening when he received a call at around eleven to tell him that Marilyn was either dying or dead and he should get over to her bungalow. Jacobs was also under instructions from 20th Century Fox to 'clean up' the scene and so present a rather sanitised version of Marilyn's so-called suicide to the press the following day. At the time Jacobs had assumed, like most others, that it was an actual suicide, but, like a good many others in Hollywood, he had come to learn different.

He admitted, almost regretfully, that because he had been working to set himself up as a film producer, his reward from the studio had been to give up his publicity company and start producing films. He was never proud of his part in the cover-up, but he never suffered the unending guilt that Peter Lawford was to feel for the rest of his life.

When Lawford revealed his part in the cover-up to the Summit, Sinatra berated him for being responsible for destroying any evidence that might have led to the real solution to Marilyn's death. Davis recalled that Frank told Lawford, 'Do you have any idea what you've done?'

Lawford was completely grief-stricken and full of guilt. 'But what else could I do?' he said.

'You could have called the police.'

'I did. There was a cop car on the scene almost immediately.'

'That isn't what the newspapers said. That isn't even what the police said.'

'That's because they were all part of it.' Lawford went on to explain that it was Los Angeles Police Chief Parker himself who assured Bobby Kennedy, after personally questioning him, that he would deal with the situation in order to keep the Kennedy name out of it. Bobby had told Parker that he was thinking of standing down as attorney general and had Parker in mind as his successor. That proved to be a powerful motivation for Parker to oblige Bobby with a complete cover-up.

Sinatra asked Lawford outright, 'Did Bobby have Marilyn killed?'

Lawford could barely put his thoughts together. He stammered that at first he did think Bobby was responsible, but that when he saw how upset Bobby was about Marilyn's death, he began to realise that Bobby couldn't have had anything to do with it.

'But it's looking like he did,' said Sinatra.

'Can't you see how it would look if Bobby's name was linked to Marilyn – how he had been to see her the day she died?' asked Lawford.

'Yeah, I can,' said Sinatra. 'So, okay, let's say Bobby didn't have her killed. Who did?'

It was becoming increasingly obvious to Sinatra that Marilyn had been murdered, and he had no reason not to suspect Sam Giancana. He told Lawford, Davis and Martin as much.

'Oh Jesus,' said Dean Martin, 'surely even Mooney wouldn't have a celebrity as big as Marilyn put down?'

Davis told me he thought Giancana would do exactly that. He said, 'He seemed perfectly capable of hitting all of us in one go over that Villa Venice scam.' The Villa Venice scam was a nefarious business venture into which Giancana would lure Sinatra, Martin and Davis in 1962.

Sinatra said that he'd felt reasonably safe from any real harm until now because of his association with Giancana, but he agreed with Davis that Mooney was becoming too dangerous to be around. 'Look, if Lucky Luciano could have Thelma Todd murdered – and we all know he did – and get away with it, why should we think the Cigar wouldn't go one better and have the biggest female star in the world taken out?'

Davis recalled how all four men talked around in circles and kept coming back to the same conclusion – that Giancana must have had Marilyn murdered. Sammy said that in that room there was 'anger, grief, confusion and fear – and a lot of tears'.

Sinatra swore his Summit to secrecy regarding his suspicions, and he set in motion, using his own personal investigators, a more thorough investigation than the Los Angeles Police Department ever carried out.

In fact, the police carried out no investigation at all, by order of Police Chief William Parker, who took it upon himself to try to bury anything that came close to the truth in order to preserve Bobby's public image. Thus the eventual theory that Bobby Kennedy had somehow been involved in Monroe's death seemed to many to have some credence. He was not the killer, nor did he give the order to have her killed, but to put him at the scene of the crime on the very day she died suited those who wanted to destroy the Kennedys.

J Edgar Hoover was sitting back and laughing quietly over Bobby Kennedy's dilemma. Neither the attorney general nor the president could afford a scandal about their relationships with Monroe which, at this time, could break so easily.

Bobby may have been responsible for ensuring that evidence was destroyed at Marilyn's home to keep him out of the picture, but he had also, in his panic, put paid to any proper investigation uncovering the real perpetrators. It would do him no good to make waves now and risk the revelations he was so desperate to keep under wraps. Nevertheless, knowing that someone had gone to a great deal of trouble to set him up, he was quietly determined to find out the truth for himself, as Lawford revealed.

Bobby was careful to carry out a low-key investigation using trusted FBI agents, and he sought Peter Lawford's help. Sinatra had told Lawford, Martin and Davis that he was almost positive that Giancana was behind Marilyn's death, and when Bobby Kennedy asked Lawford for his ongoing support to find out who killed Monroe – partly, selfishly, to clear himself – Lawford suggested that Sinatra 'might be worth questioning'.

Frank was furious to find himself being interrogated by FBI agents. They came to him in secrecy and promised him immunity from anything he might say that could incriminate him in any way as far as his associations with the Mafia were concerned. At this time, Sinatra had nothing more to go on than a well-educated guess about Marilyn's death, but he was not going to start suggesting to federal agents that Sam Giancana might be behind the murder.

The agents left Sinatra with a friendly suggestion that if he should discover anything, the attorney general would welcome his co-operation. He flew into a rage, furious at having been put in that position – and he suspected Lawford was behind it. Lawford told me – and Davis confirmed it – that Sinatra confronted him, and he sheepishly admitted that he had suggested that Bobby send agents to question Frank. He insisted he was only doing what he thought right. Sinatra disagreed. *That* was when he told Lawford he would never speak to him again.

That was the cause of the rift that lasted for the rest of Lawford's life, and because he could never reveal his involvement in the conspiracy over Marilyn's death – or the truth he and the others later came to know – he could never give the true explanation why Sinatra abolished him from the Summit for all time. Thus, Lawford himself was instrumental in creating the myth that he became *persona non grata* to Sinatra when he told Frank that the president had changed his mind about staying at his Palm Springs home. It was a far more plausible story, with none of the unfortunate or unpleasant consequences that the truth would hold in store for the concerned many.

Joe DiMaggio made the funeral arrangements for Marilyn, and he drew up a list of those who could attend and those who couldn't. Among those on the blacklist were Peter and Pat Lawford, Dean Martin and Frank Sinatra. 'DiMaggio always felt they were all in some way responsible for Marilyn's death,' said Ava. 'He didn't know Frank was going to find out who was really responsible.'

For almost two months Sinatra's private investigation continued. Finally he told friends, 'I don't think I need to know what happened, after all. What's the point? It's not gonna bring her back, is it?'

Secretly, however, he had discovered the truth. Exactly how, neither Davis, nor Lawford, nor Ava could explain – but all three confirmed each other's story that Frank Sinatra discovered who killed Marilyn, and how, and why.

As Frank had feared, Marilyn Monroe had sealed her fate that weekend at the Cal-Neva when she drunkenly confided to Sam Giancana. She had broken the golden rule of the Mafia, even though she was not a part of the Mafia. She was, nevertheless, involved, and when you're in that precarious position, you never try to walk away – and, more importantly, you never talk. That was exactly what she had threatened to do.

It has been suggested that Monroe had found herself acting as a go-between for Giancana and the Kennedys. No mention of that was ever made to me. Yet she knew, probably through Bobby Kennedy, more than was healthy for her to know. What she knew was enough, were she to carry out her threat, to harm the plans of the Mafia and a faction of the CIA who had reason for wanting the president out of office – but only in their own good time. Giancana saw it as an opportunity to bring scandal to the White House once and for all, as well as dealing with someone 'prepared to squeal', as Ava put it.

Through Johnny Roselli, Giancana made contact with CIA agents and briefed them on the situation. It was decided that they could take no risks – and that meant Marilyn Monroe had to die.

Johnny Roselli summoned assassins – probably three – who arrived in Los Angeles from various destinations on Saturday 4 August 1962. Giancana had been told by his CIA contacts that Bobby Kennedy would be in Los Angeles that same day, and they all agreed that, with a certain amount of planning and luck, the attorney general himself might somehow become implicated. Whether he did or not didn't really matter. They figured that, when Monroe's body was found, a thorough investigation would reveal at the very least that Bobby Kennedy had been involved with Marilyn

Monroe. To be sure of that, certain evidence would be placed at the scene by the killers, to be discovered later by the police.

That evening Roselli went to Marilyn's bungalow. She was still in a state of sedation from the injection given to her that afternoon. Because she knew Roselli and trusted him, she saw no reason not to let him in. The hit men quickly followed him through the front door, grabbed Marilyn and easily overpowered her. The fact that she was sedated made it all the easier. (Exactly what Eunice Murray was doing at this time, or how much she saw, will never be known because she is now dead. She did, however, reveal towards the end of her life that the events as reported by the police, based on statements made by her, Dr Engelberg and Dr Greenson, were false.) They dragged Marilyn to her bedroom and inserted a suppository soaked with Nembutal barbiturate into her rectum. The massive dose quickly entered her bloodstream, and from that moment there was no chance of saving her.

When Frank Sinatra received this report, he swore vengeance on the man who had ordered the contract – Sam Giancana. In fact, it had come to Giancana's notice that Sinatra had investigators asking questions, and from what Ava told me, Frank himself was not slow to ask sly questions of both Giancana and Roselli in the hope of learning something.

When Sinatra got wind that Giancana was wondering why he had become so nosy, Frank prudently let it be known that he was calling off the investigation and that he thought it pointless to continue. It seemed to him that this allayed Giancana's concerns, but neither man would ever completely trust the other again. There began an ongoing game in which both men went out of their way to give the impression to each other that all was well between them – but each was secretly laying the foundation of the other's downfall. It was, in every sense, a vendetta that would take time to reach fruition.

Chapter Twelve

Vendetta

Giancana had built a new nightclub, the Villa Venice in Wheeling, just outside Chicago, and nearby he had built a secret illegal casino. He spent 250,000 dollars on the place, and because he could not put his own name on the deeds as owner, he gave a man called Leo Olson the job of managing the establishment.

Sam wanted the best entertainers in the world to bring in the rich punters who, after the show, would literally be shuttled to the casino where they were guaranteed to lose vast amounts of money at the tables.

The Villa Venice opened in October 1962, with Eddie Fisher playing to a packed house. Fisher had not wanted to open the place, but he had been persuaded by Sinatra to do it because, said Fisher, 'He asked me on the day Marilyn had died, and Frank was too upset to even think about performing.' Fisher argued that he had been working hard at the Latin Casino, and was due to play the Winter Garden and then the Desert Inn, which would simply mean he wasn't available to do the Villa Venice. Frank did not give up, so Fisher told him that, if he was really needed, someone would have to get him out of his contract with the Desert Inn. Fisher thought that would be an end to the matter, because the Desert Inn was a direct competitor to the Sands, which was part-owned by Sinatra, and there was no way the Desert Inn would let him go for the sake of Sinatra. To Fisher's surprise, however, Frank did manage somehow to arrange for the Desert Inn to release Fisher, and he became the entertainer who opened the notorious Villa Venice.

Sinatra did subsequently play there, and so did Sammy Davis and Dean Martin. They performed individually and then together as the Summit, just as the Rat Pack had done at the Sands in Las Vegas.

The FBI had been keeping tabs on the progress of the Villa Venice and they knew that Giancana was behind it, but they needed evidence. On opening night, Eddie Fisher found federal agents coming into his dressing room and grilling him to find out what he could tell them about who really ran the club. Fisher explained that he didn't know Sam Giancana and couldn't tell them whether or not he owned the place. In fact, Fisher complained that he was being paid 'next to nothing', and the agents demanded to know why he was performing there. He replied that he had been asked to by 'a friend'.

During the opening night, Giancana was introduced to Fisher as 'Dr Goldberg'. At the time Fisher didn't know who he was. He said, 'He didn't strike me as a typical Jewish doctor.' Curiously, in his autobiography, Eddie Fisher described Giancana as 'a warm, vital, funny man', which was hardly the way Ava Gardner viewed Mooney. Giancana simply didn't like entertainers, with Frank Sinatra having once been the exception, but Fisher had the impression that he and Sam the Cigar became 'very close friends'. He said that Giancana treated him like 'the Jewish son he never had'.

One of Giancana's girlfriends, the singer Phyllis McGuire, had been in business with Eddie Fisher, running a music publishing company. As he got to know Giancana better, Fisher saw how tempestuous his affair with Phyllis was. Sam once advised him never to give a woman a gun. He told Fisher, 'I got Phyllis this little gold-plated Beretta to keep in her pocketbook. A couple of days later she's chasing me down the street with it.'

The night Fisher met him at the Villa Venice, Dr Goldberg was with Judith Campbell Exner, who was, as it happened, a girlfriend of Fisher's (his marriage to Liz Taylor had ended when she took up with her *Cleopatra* co-star Richard Burton). When he eventually realised that Dr Goldberg was really Sam Giancana, the boss of the Chicago Mafia, Fisher decided to play safe and not get too friendly with Judith. Yet Giancana encouraged him to date Judith, insisting that he take her to dinners and parties when Sam was too busy to accompany her. To make sure Fisher behaved himself with Judith, Giancana always sent one of his men to act as a chaperon. Fisher said, 'Believe me, I behaved.'

The name of Judith Campbell Exner has become inextricably linked with those of Frank Sinatra, Jack Kennedy and Sam Giancana. A professional party girl, she had once been Sinatra's girlfriend. They had begun their affair in November 1959, while holidaying in Hawaii along with the Lawfords. By February 1960 their affair was at an end, and Frank was happy to introduce Judith to Jack Kennedy. She became one of the then senator's many bedmates. Barely a week after her affair with Kennedy had begun, Sinatra invited her to see him perform at the Fontainebleau in Miami, and there he introduced her to 'Sam Flood' – who turned out to be none other than Sam Giancana. Judith embarked on an affair with the gangster while still seeing Jack Kennedy. Sam thereafter got a kick out of knowing that he and the president of the United States were sharing the same girlfriend.

Eddie Fisher noted that even though Giancana was a Catholic as well as a married man, none of that stopped him from asking Judith to marry him several times. When she finally told him, 'Yes,' he simply replied, 'Fuck off!'

Judith would later claim that she passed messages between

Giancana and the president, but Eddie Fisher doubted that this was true. Nonetheless, there was certainly a tangled web in which Eddie got a little caught up. He was later introduced by Pat Newcomb to Pamela Turnure, Jackie Kennedy's press secretary. One evening Giancana caught up with Fisher and Turnure, and told her, 'There are the good guys and the bad guys in this world and a nice young lady like you should be careful about who you're with.' Fisher assumed that this was a joke at his expense, but Giancana may have been referring to something that was to happen in the not-too-distant future: Pam Turnure was with Jackie and Jack Kennedy in Dallas on the day the president was assassinated.

Sammy Davis recalled that when he appeared at the Villa Venice, he was also questioned by the FBI. He was careful to tell them nothing that could implicate him or the others in what was essentially 'a sucker plan set by Sam, plain and simple', as Lawford would later comment.

The Villa Venice closed after a month, not because of failure, but because that had always been Giancana's plan – something of which Sinatra had not been aware. Mooney made three million dollars tax free, and with that, he had the casino bulldozed to the ground and the nightclub closed indefinitely. It never opened again.

Sinatra had the good sense to maintain that none of the entertainers who worked at the club did so under any kind of threat, and Dean Martin later reported that he performed there simply because he was well paid. Sammy Davis, however, told me that this was an engagement they had all agreed to do 'with reluctance', not least because none of them were actually paid for their services. They all owed Giancana – and would do for life – and they all had to oblige.

Sammy Davis remembered the occasion when he, Dean Martin and Sinatra were summoned for a meeting with Giancana. 'We dreaded going because, by this time, we all wanted out from being in debt to that guy.'

Giancana told them that they were all to play the Villa Venice. Davis said, 'I don't know if you know this, but in his early days Dean tried his hand at being a bit of a gangster, but he wasn't cut out for it. He was too nice a guy. He's gentle and sweet. You have to love him. But he didn't like Sam Mooney telling him what to do.'

Martin told Giancana, 'Why the hell would I want to play the Villa Venice?'

'Because I fucking told you to,' said Giancana.

Dean, thoughtfully and quietly, argued, 'Let's take a look at the situation, Sam. You *need* us. I ain't so sure we need you.'

Giancana was fuming, but tried to keep control of his temper. Davis said he knew that Giancana could snuff out Dean's life with a single order to one of his men. Giancana said, 'What's all this fucking shit I'm getting from you? Frank, you tell him; he's your fucking friend.'

Before Sinatra could say anything, Martin said, 'Don't do me the discourtesy of talking about me like I wasn't here. You talk to me. If Sammy and Frank want to do the show, that's up to them. But I ain't tied down to either Sammy or Frank – or you – by any contract. So let's talk business.'

'What fucking business? I'm telling you what the business is. I want the three of you to play the Villa Venice. We don't fucking negotiate.'

'But I *am* negotiating, Mr Giancana. I want to know what's in it for us. How much are you gonna pay us to play your hotel?'

Giancana was, by now, ready to explode. 'I don't have to pay you a fucking nickel. You owe me, all of you, and I'm calling in your fucking debts.'

'Now hold on,' said Dean. 'I don't owe you nothing. You show me the IOU with my name on it.'

Giancana whipped out a gun and aimed it at Martin, saying, 'Here's your fucking IOU.'

Sinatra had been growing more nervous as Dean argued with Giancana, and he finally said, 'Dean, for God's sake, let's just do the fucking show.'

'Are you gonna do it?' Dean asked him.

'Of course I'm gonna do it,' said Frank.

'What about you, Sammy?'

Sammy had no desire to get his head blown off. He said, 'Me? Yeah! Sure! Okay!'

Davis told me, 'I don't know if Giancana would have shot us all dead there and then, but I sure as hell wasn't taking no chance. Later Dean said to me, "He wouldn't have killed us – three top entertainers, all found dead. He'd never have got away with it." I told Dean, "Maybe, but if he *had* killed us, I wouldn't have had the satisfaction of knowing the son of a bitch wouldn't have got away with it."'

It became the policy of the Summit to claim that they had been paid well.

Frank told Ava that he and his Summit performed at the Villa Venice because Giancana told them to. Sinatra resented being so obligated to Giancana and had, in the past, managed to avoid some of the favours he'd been asked to do. At that time, however, he was particularly keen not to upset Mooney following his death threat – which is why he not only persuaded Eddie Fisher to play the Villa Venice when Giancana told him that was who he wanted, but had reluctantly agreed to perform there himself. He didn't earn a cent from any of it, and he grew ever more bitter at continually having to show his gratitude to Giancana for past favours. More than that, he wanted to get revenge for the death of Marilyn. He promised himself that it would all come to an end between him and Giancana – one way or another.

*

Ever since Sinatra had reneged on some of his promises to Giancana, the Mafia boss of the Chicago Outfit had been quietly laying the foundation for what he planned would be Sinatra's eventual downfall. The FBI knew Frank was involved with Giancana, and so did the Kennedys. Sam the Cigar had envisioned the day when he and Sinatra would no longer have to pretend to be friends. That's what they had both been doing, ever since Frank had received the skinned head of a lamb: just playing the game of friendship because it was prudent to do so. All this time, however, Giancana had been laying the foundation that would give Sinatra a reputation as a suspected killer.

Before Marilyn Monroe was murdered, an incident had occurred that was to cast suspicion on Sinatra as a cold-blooded killer that persists even today. There was a girl who worked at the Cal-Neva who, for a time, was Sinatra's girlfriend. Then she married the local deputy sheriff, Dick Anderson. One night Anderson arrived at the Cal-Neva to collect his wife, and an argument ensued between him and Sinatra. No one knows what it was about, but it ended with the deputy sheriff punching Sinatra in the mouth, causing him an injury that prevented him from singing for several days.

About a week later, Anderson and his wife were driving up a winding cliff road. Conditions were dry, and the cliffs were to the left of Anderson, who drove on the right-hand side. A car overtook them and then slowed down, forcing Anderson to overtake. As he did so, the other car pulled over, ramming Anderson's car hard and forcing it over the edge. It rolled down and smashed into trees. Anderson was killed but his wife survived. The wreck was quickly sent to the breaker's yard to be crushed into a little box, and all files regarding the matter mysteriously disappeared. Sinatra was the prime suspect.

It turned out that Sinatra had spoken to his Cal-Neva partner Skinny D'Amato and said that he wanted the deputy sheriff to have 'a little scare'. D'Amato was believed by the FBI to be one of Giancana's 'enforcers', and as such he was at Frank's disposal. So D'Amato arranged for the incident, which, as far as Frank was concerned, was not supposed to end so tragically. What Frank didn't know then – although he found out later – was that D'Amato had had words with Giancana about it, and Giancana had said, 'Just kill the fucking guy.' D'Amato was not in a position to protest, although it seems he was unhappy with the whole plan because he really was a good friend of Frank.

He carried out the plan nonetheless. Then, with a few kickbacks, D'Amato was able to make sure any evidence was removed, his intent being to make it look as if there was a cover-up – which there was. The cover-up was all part of Giancana's plan to frame Sinatra.

'Frank could be a dangerous bastard,' Ava told me. 'He never hurt me, although we had plenty of fights – but he was never violent.'

Sammy Davis said, 'If you crossed Frank, he could put the fear of God into you, and as much as I love the guy, to me his methods leave a lot to be desired.'

There is a story about an incident that once took place on Sinatra's private aeroplane. Frank ordered his valet of twenty years' service, George Jacobs, to get him a hard-boiled egg. Jacobs mistakenly picked out a raw egg and brought it to Frank, who had a girl sitting on his lap. As Sinatra opened it, the egg went all over him and the girl.

Sinatra flew into one of his famous tempers, got up, grabbed Jacobs, dragged him to the door and flung it open. Dean Martin, who luckily was on board, rushed over and got Sinatra into a headlock while someone else pulled Jacobs clear of the door.

Davis told me, 'Who knows if he would have thrown George out? Personally, I don't believe he would have, but it scared the shit out of poor George. Thanks to Dino, we'll never know. But

I can't see Frank, even at his worst, killing his trusted valet George.'

At his worst, Sinatra could certainly be a dangerous force to reckon with – 'Not one of his most endearing qualities,' said Ava.

One night he went to see a young comedian, Jackie Mason, performing in Las Vegas. Sinatra was drunk, which brought out the worst in him, and he began abusing Mason from where he sat. Mason wasn't going to take that, even from Frank Sinatra, and abused him in turn from the stage.

A few nights later, Mason was in his dressing room when a hail of bullets smashed through his window. He could only guess that this was Sinatra's way of paying him back. Mason then made the mistake of making jokes about Sinatra during his act. A few days later he was confronted by a couple of men, one of whom wore a horrific ring which had a blade attached to it. He punched Mason, cutting his nose and putting him out of business for several weeks. He was told, 'Now will you stop abusing Mr Sinatra?'

Did Sinatra give the order to put the frighteners on Mason and inflict such violence upon him? The impression I got from Ava and Sammy Davis was that he was perfectly capable of doing just that. He used Mafia-style tactics on those who offended him – but they insisted he would never have gone as far as having anyone killed. At least, they didn't know of anyone who had been killed either by him or on his orders. Yet I do remember Sammy saying, 'But you never know.'

Even if Sinatra was capable of killing, could he be capable of killing Sam Giancana? He certainly had the means to do it, and the motive. However, I think the fact that he found another way to avenge the death of Monroe, as well as other grievances he had against the Mafia boss, demonstrates that Sinatra was not a violent thug, as many have portrayed him, but a clever manager of his own sense of justice.

Sammy Davis explained, 'You can't figure Frank out. He

wasn't a bad guy – I mean, not like Dr Goldberg. He was basically a good guy who did a lot of good things: things you never hear about. And, yeah, he did some bad stuff, man.'

The good things that no one knew about – which means that the newspapers never got wind of any of it – were his many charitable acts. There are many celebrities who are generous with their time and money, and some of them prefer to keep quiet about it, while others make a point of generating publicity from it. Sinatra was keen to keep many of his charitable acts private. Only when he put on properly organised benefit concerts did he receive publicity, but he never sought it.

When Janet Leigh told him about a family she had heard of who were poor and had no food or presents for Christmas, she suggested he might put on a benefit show to raise funds for them. Sinatra had also heard about this particular family, and he told her, 'There are presents, food and clothing already on their way by plane.' There was no need for a benefit show, no need for publicity. It was simply something he felt should be done, all paid for by him. If Janet Leigh had not revealed that particular event, which she did after Sinatra's death just to demonstrate his generosity, no one would have known about it.

So we are left with an image of a man who was caring, who could be a good friend, but who also could be a fearful enemy. He was, in the classic sense, a man of the Mafia – and that simply comes from his breeding and his background. That is why there are people who hated him, and plenty more who adored him.

Sam Giancana had to be aware of Sinatra's capabilities, which was why, step by step, he was looking to cripple him. Giancana was sure that one day – probably on the day he might well be called to pay the penalty for his own crimes – Frank Sinatra would be revealed and condemned as a man who was almost as much a mafioso as Sam the Cigar.

Sinatra's salvation, however, was his ability as an actor. He could lie convincingly, which was why he always managed to wriggle out of the numerous tight spots he found himself in when being questioned about his Mafia associations. He also lied to Giancana, keeping up the pretence of being his friend, while all the time he was looking for that opportunity to bring Giancana down.

The FBI continued to investigate Sam Giancana throughout 1962. Giancana was clever, though, and made sure Bobby Kennedy learned that he had tapes to prove that Bobby and Jack had both been involved with Marilyn Monroe. Kennedy thereafter made attempts to retrieve those tapes.

The paradox of the whole situation was that the CIA, or a faction of it, were trying to protect the Mafia and destroy the Kennedys, while the FBI, which Bobby Kennedy had been gradually wrestling from Hoover's once-iron grip, was trying to make sure that Bobby was never implicated in Monroe's murder in any way. The cover-up simply fuelled suspicions that Bobby was responsible for Marilyn's death, a theory that has now gone past its sell-by date and should be ditched by even the most thorough of the investigators who still pursue the matter.

As Ava put it, 'The Kennedys were good people, and the president was a good president. Their only crime was the same one too many men I've known commit, if you must call it a crime – women. I guess that was Frank's crime too.'

Crime or not, Ava decided to give Frank another chance. After she had finished filming *55 Days at Peking*, she met with him. Where they met, I don't recall her ever saying, but he revealed to her that his suspicions about Giancana having Monroe killed were correct. She begged him to tread carefully. 'I tell you, he was going to punish Giancana one way or another,' she said to me.

He also told her that he still loved her and needed her – despite the many other affairs he would have had going on at the time.

They talked things over and agreed to give their relationship another try. In the summer of 1963 Ava temporarily moved out of her villa in Madrid and into Frank's New York apartment. He declared to friends, 'I'm the happiest man in the world.'

And they were happy – for a short while. The trouble was, Ava admitted, that neither of them had learned their lessons, and before long they were fighting again. She said that the old problem about his mobster friends had not gone away. She particularly hated Sam Giancana, especially now that she knew he had ordered the death of Monroe.

'I warned him that his so-called friends would destroy him. I was scared about what he would eventually do to Giancana. I had visions of there one day being a shoot-out, and I'd get killed, and he'd get killed. I often woke up in the night drenched in perspiration from dreams about it. I did for years after.'

Sinatra tried to reassure her that nothing of the sort would ever happen. 'Sam thinks everything is sweet,' he told her. The truth was, though, he was nervous that she might be right. He knew that Giancana had his suspicions, but he didn't want Ava worrying.

Ava recalled how, during this reconciliation, the only place she felt safe was at the house of Frank's mother Dolly. She knew no mobster would dare to touch anyone there. One day Dolly cooked a big meal for Ava and Frank. Joining them for dinner was Phyllis McGuire. Ava knew she was a girlfriend of Giancana's, and asked her pointedly, 'Aren't you scared of these people you hang around with?'

'What are you talking about?' replied Phyllis.

Ava told her in a way that just left Phyllis speechless. 'Don't act innocent with me, sister, because it doesn't wash with me. And it won't wash with the FBI, either.'

One night Ava and Frank were at Jilly's, a bar restaurant on West 52nd Street owned by Sinatra's friend Jilly Rizzo, when Giancana came in and joined them. Frank put on a great act as he declared, 'Look, Ava, it's my best pal Sam!' Ava scowled at Giancana. As Giancana sat down, she stood up and walked over to a man sitting alone at a table, and sat on his lap.

'I don't know why I did that,' she admitted to me. 'I wanted to make it a slap in the face for Giancana, but all I did was slap Frank's face. Bad mistake!'

Frank stormed over and pushed her off the stranger's lap, then grabbed the man by the lapels and hauled him to his feet, telling him, 'You're lucky I don't kill you.' He shoved the poor mystified and frightened man into his chair, then grabbed Ava's arm to drag her back to her seat and push her back into it.

Ava was not one to be pushed around by Frank. She stood up again, and announced, 'How dare you? I'm leaving.'

He forced her back into the chair, yelling, 'The hell you are!'

Giancana looked on, saying, 'You gonna let her get away with that?'

She recalled how she wanted, there and then, to tell Giancana exactly what she thought of him and that she knew he'd had Monroe killed. 'I came so close,' she told me. 'It wasn't Frank I was mad at – I was used to him shoving me around and me shoving him back – but I really despised that fucking no-good hood.'

Frank told Ava, 'Apologise to Sam.' But she just stared coldly at the gangster, and then left the restaurant.

Giancana just laughed. 'She got no respect for you,' he told Sinatra.

The very next day Ava moved all her belongings out of Frank's apartment, and went back to Spain. It was their last attempt at a reunion. She told me, 'I think I could have put up with the fights a little longer because the making-up was always so good. But I couldn't stand living in fear, although I was always afraid for Frank.'

For ever after they remained friends, however, and they kept in touch by phone. Frank would call her from whichever country he happened to be in, and he kept her informed of his progress with the vendetta.

Sam Giancana was forbidden by Nevada law to enter any casino in the state. The FBI had been keeping a close eye on the Cal-Neva, and noted that Giancana had entered the premises on the Nevada side of the border from 17 July to 28 July 1963. This was reported to the Nevada State Gaming Board and led to Sinatra being called before the Licensing Control Board.

He was questioned about Giancana's visits and, faced with the evidence the FBI had supplied, Sinatra was unable to deny it. He simply explained that Giancana had visited the lodge, but that he had no personal or professional dealings with him. It was enough, however, for the board to file charges against Frank in September 1963 for allowing Giancana onto the premises.

Sinatra knew he was about to lose his gaming licence. Deciding to face up to the fact, he announced in October that he was giving up both his gaming licence and the Cal-Neva. It also meant that he would lose his nine-per-cent interest in the Sands, so he sold his casino shares and bought stocks in Warner Bros.

As he knew would happen, the Gaming Board formally revoked his licence. It was a bitter blow, but he saw this as a way of breaking free from Sam Giancana as a business associate once and for all.

In November of 1963, Sinatra's son, Frank, was kidnapped by Barry Keenan and Joe Amsler for a ransom. The anxiety Frank had suffered at the time of the Kefauver investigation into organised crime was nothing compared with what he now went through.

He was genuinely touched when Bobby Kennedy personally called and offered the FBI's help, which Frank accepted gracefully and gratefully.

Then he got another offer of help – from someone he wanted no help from. It was Sam Giancana.

Sinatra didn't want any Mafia involvement, least of all from Giancana, and he told him, 'I'm letting the FBI handle this.'

According to Ava, Giancana said to him, 'What the fuck is this? I offer you my fucking help and you show such fucking disrespect!'

Frank kept as cool as he could and said, 'Please, Sam, let me do things my way.'

The FBI did indeed find Frank Jr, who had been held by his captors for fifty-four hours – by which time Frank Sr was ill with worry. He was pleased when Bobby Kennedy called again, just to see how he and his son were.

Then Giancana called him. 'I'm glad you got your son back,' he said, 'but I'm pissed off with you.'

'What the hell for?'

'Because I offer you my fucking help and all you say is "Fuck you".'

'Sam, I never said "Fuck you", but you know what? Fuck you!'

'Well I say fuck you! Who do you think you are, talking like that? You're gonna fucking regret it, I promise you.'

After what he had just been through, Frank felt no fear – although he should have done. He felt suddenly free of Giancana once and for all, and decided it was time to rebuild his relationship with the president. But on 22 November 1963, John F Kennedy was assassinated in Dallas.

Chapter Thirteen

A Secret Pact

After the death of the president, Bobby Kennedy ceased operations to bust organised crime. Sinatra, shocked and sickened, sent the Kennedy family his personal condolences. But show business being what it is, he got straight back to work, making use of his stock in Warner Bros to make the next Summit picture, *Robin and the Seven Hoods*. It was a musical spoof on the gangster genre, loosely based on the Robin Hood legend. Sammy Davis said it was Frank's way at thumbing his nose at Sam Giancana in a way that was so subtle that even Giancana didn't recognise 'a picture that was intended to make the Outfit look risible'.

Giancana apparently found the film 'a fucking pile of shit', and asked Sinatra, 'Is that what you think we are? Modern-day Robin Hoods? You must have your fucking head stuck up your fucking ass.'

Sinatra would have liked to have told Giancana that he was the only one with his head up his ass, but instead expressed feigned disappointment that Sam had not been entertained by it.

'Frank got a kick out of sending up the Mob,' said Davis, 'but many in the Mob loved it. They thought, "Hey, Frank's letting everyone know we really care." They were all too dumb to see the point.'

This was the first of the Summit films not to feature Peter Lawford, a man Sammy Davis still liked. To prove it, he later made two films with him, *Salt and Pepper* and its sequel *One More Time*. The latter was directed by Jerry Lewis, Dean Martin's one-time screen and stage partner.

'I always felt like the peacemaker,' Davis told me in 1974. 'On the one hand I loved Frank and I loved Peter, but Frank hated Peter and Peter hated Frank – or so they claim. I'll tell you this – Frank misses Peter, and vice versa. And on the other hand I love Dean and I like Jerry Lewis, and they're supposed to hate each other too. Don't you believe it. They never see each other, never speak, but I know they miss each other. But somehow I can't get them all together the way I want to – which would certainly make my life easier.'

In the early 1960s, Sinatra was at his professional peak with both his music and his films. He kept himself as busy as he could with movies, but in the back of his mind he was still formulating his plan to bring down Sam Giancana.

He eventually decided on a secret plan, and only a very few ever knew about it. Among those were Sammy Davis, Dean Martin and Ava Gardner, in whom he confided the most personal of secrets.

'He could tell me,' she said, 'because I was one of the few people he knew he could trust, and who wouldn't be affected by any unfortunate outcome – like getting shot fucking dead. In fact, he only ever told me what he'd been up to after the fact. He knew, if he told me his plans before he did them, I'd only nag him because I'd be scared to death *he'd* be the one to be shot fucking dead. That's one reason, I guess, I still love the fucking dumb...' She never finished that sentence, because she began to cry.

As far as Sammy Davis was concerned, 'Anything that got us free from the Mob was okay by me. Just so long as getting free didn't mean getting dead.'

Getting dead was a distinct possibility. Sam Giancana had a network of hoods who were able to find out anything and everything that might affect him. In this, Sinatra may have been careless, because Giancana received word from Johnny Roselli that Frank was up to something.

'I say, let's take the whole fucking lot of them out,' urged Roselli. 'Sinatra, the nigger and Martin. We don't need 'em any more. I tell you, they know something about Marilyn and if we ain't careful, they'll bring the Feds down on us.'

Giancana was less fearful than Roselli, but he was concerned. 'I got a better idea. Send another message to Sinatra. Let him know he can't fuck us, or he will be dead.'

Giancana not only underestimated Sinatra, but he failed to realise that his own network was not as watertight as he thought. Somehow, news of this conversation reached Sinatra.

Not long after, Frank received another skinned head of a lamb.

'Fuck this,' he said angrily (according to Davis), knowing it was just another idle threat. 'I'll sort Giancana out once and for all.'

He set his plan in motion. He asked Davis to speak to Lawford and arrange for a secret meeting with Bobby Kennedy. Davis suggested, 'Peter might not feel inclined to help out, considering you said you never wanted to see him again.'

Frank, conceited enough to think that Lawford would drop everything to make himself a part of the Summit once more, said, 'Tell Peter if he does this, everything'll be all right between us.'

So Davis went to see Lawford, who asked why he should do anything for Frank after the way he'd been treated. Davis told him that this might be the way to put Giancana out of action once and for all – and it might patch things up between Lawford and Sinatra.

Lawford was, by now, uninterested in a friendship with someone who had twice expelled him. He said, 'As far as I'm concerned, Frank can go fuck himself. But if it puts that weasel [Giancana] out of action, I'll see what I can do.'

The meeting was arranged, and Bobby met Frank to hear what he had to say. Sinatra laid his cards on the table. He said he knew Bobby could put him away for his associations with the Mafia, and he appreciated the fact that Bobby had always kept his promise not to make any attempt to incriminate him. He also knew, he said, that Giancana had not only had Marilyn killed, but that he had timed the murder to coincide with Bobby's visit to Lawford's house that weekend in the hope of either incriminating the Kennedys in the killing or, at the very least, exposing his and his brother's relationships with Marilyn.

Bobby said that none of this was exactly news to him: his own investigations had revealed as much. When Frank asked him why he'd done nothing about it, Bobby explained that, had he done so, he would have exposed himself and his late brother to scandal.

In the course of their conversation, Bobby opened up and confessed how much he regretted what had happened to Marilyn and how he felt guilty and powerless at being unable to bring Giancana to justice. Frank understood. According to Ava, tears flowed from both men's eyes, not only for Marilyn, but for Jack too. Bobby never publicly expressed his conviction that the assassination of his brother had been a conspiracy between the CIA and the Mafia, and possibly high-ranking officials in the military, or that Sam Giancana and Johnny Roselli had been instrumental in organising elements of the actual shooting. But in private, to Sinatra, he revealed all this and more.

Bobby had also confided his suspicions to a few who were close to him. One of those few was his aide Larry O'Brien. Bobby told him, 'I'm sure that little pinko prick [Fidel Castro] had something to do with it, but he certainly didn't mastermind anything.' Shortly after the president's assassination, Bobby contacted John McCone at the CIA and asked what the CIA knew about the assassination, and whether the CIA itself could have been involved. McCone actually suggested it could have been the Mafia. Bobby told him, 'They should have killed me. I'm the one they wanted.'

When the Warren Commission, set up to investigate the president's murder, finally announced that Lee Harvey Oswald had acted alone in killing Jack Kennedy, and that Jack Ruby – who shot Oswald dead following his arrest – had also acted alone, Bobby told LaVern Duffy, one of his organised-crime investigators, that it was 'impossible that Oswald and Ruby hadn't known one another'. He also told Duffy, 'Those Cuban cunts are all working for the Mob. They blame us for the Bay of Pigs, and they're trying to make this look like a Castro–Communist hit. I don't buy it. And I don't trust those guys at the CIA. They're worse than the Mafia.'

Publicly, he withdrew from any suggestion or hint of an investigation into his brother's death. He even disbanded the Organized Crime Task Force, and must have felt powerless, admitting defeat even to those closest to him. LaVern Duffy claimed, 'Bobby simply didn't want to know who did it. But at the same time, he couldn't put it behind him. He wanted to bring his brother's murderers to justice, but he didn't have the strength to do it. He must have felt tremendous guilt over his failure to act.'

It wasn't until May 1997 that former President Gerald Ford admitted that in 1975, while he was in office, he had received reports indicating that Johnny Roselli and Carlos Marcello had orchestrated the assassination plot. Ford had suppressed these reports, which had been based on FBI and CIA files.)

At the time, Bobby told Sinatra that he was indeed powerless to do anything about it. His plan was to run for president himself, after standing down as attorney general, and, once in the White House, he would find a way to bring out the facts concerning the plot to kill Jack.

It was an emotional meeting during which Frank said that he would provide Bobby with all the details he needed to put Giancana away, provided that Bobby promised him not only immunity but total anonymity. They shook hands, and a deal was made. Now the conspiracy was set against Sam Giancana – and what eventually pleased Frank the most was that Giancana never knew anything about it. This was one secret Sinatra was able to keep even from the most cunning of Giancana's spies.

Just how many knew about all this is never likely to be known. Certainly Ava knew it, and so did Sammy Davis Jr. Sinatra's attorney, Mickey Rudin, may have known, but if he did he never let on. I don't believe any of his family knew. According to Davis, Sinatra let Ava in on it because he wanted her to know, after all their many arguments over his Mob associations, that he was seeking some kind of redemption. He trusted Ava with his life, said Davis, and she was just distant enough in those days to be out of harm's way, should harm come to him. He always felt bad, said Davis, that he had put Ava through so much trauma in their early days – especially the day when the mobsters came and smashed his place up and Ava thought they were both going to die.

Davis was in on it because he was always so close to Sinatra, who needed a confidant. Dean Martin also knew, for the same reasons. The difference between Sammy and Dean was that Sammy was always alarmed about the whole deal, while Martin simply had the attitude, 'Let's get the bastard once and for all.'

'It was like a conspiracy being hatched,' Davis recounted to me. 'We'd sit and talk, and we never offered up ideas or suggestions because Frank simply told us what he was doing and what he was going to do and what he hoped it would achieve. I'd sit there and go, "Oh, man, if Sam finds out, you're dead, man," while Dean just sat back and said, "He [Giancana] deserves all he gets."'

Sammy said that it was never a case of Frank calling them together for some kind of secret meeting to discuss his vendetta.

'We just kinda talked about it when we were together,' said Davis. Sometimes it would just be Frank and Sammy, sometimes Frank and Dean, and sometimes the three of them together. Neither Sammy nor Dean ever brought the subject up. If there was news, Frank would tell them.

One day Dean asked Frank, 'Do you have to let us in on everything? This ain't really none of our business. This is your vendetta.'

Frank replied, 'Who the hell else am I gonna tell? Do you have any idea what a cross this is to bear? All by myself?'

'Sure, Frank, but you made the cross for yourself.'

That angered Frank. He said, 'I'm doing this for all of us, for Christ's sake. Us and Marilyn. You wanna let Sam get away with what he did?'

Sammy said that Dean didn't answer. He just went quiet. Sammy guessed that Dean had to be in agreement with Frank, because he knew he was right. As for Sammy, he offered to do anything he could, and on a number of occasions asked Sinatra if there was anything he could do. He admitted to me that he only asked because he wanted to show solidarity with the man who had turned his life around and given him all the support he needed when he needed it most – when he lost his eye and his confidence. He was always relieved when Frank told him, 'Nah, you don't have to do anything, Sammy, except be there for me.'

'I'll always be there for you, Frank.'

Sammy said that all he ever had to do was listen to Frank outline what his next move was, or hear reports on whatever had recently happened. That's all Frank wanted from both Sammy and Dean, and that's what they gave him.

One day Frank told them, 'Unless I wind up getting myself killed over this, no one's ever gonna know that I tried to do the right thing. If that happens, you two will know.'

Sammy asked, 'You mean, you want us to be the ones to tell

the world what you did – if you wind up dead, that is?'

'That's for you to decide, Sammy. You and Dean, at least, will know. You both mean as much to me as my own family, and I'm never gonna tell them – not as long as I'm alive. And, by the way, I intend to stay alive. So just humour me, guys, and be my witnesses. If this comes off, and I live through this, no one else need ever know. And if I get bumped off in the process... Well, I leave it to you.'

Then Dean, ever the cynic, asked, 'Yeah, but what happens if we *all* get bumped off in the process?'

'Jesus, Dean,' said Frank, 'try and be positive.'

'Oh, I'm positive,' replied Dean. 'I'm positive I don't want to get bumped off.'

As for Peter Lawford, Davis said he must have known some of what Frank was up to because of his relations to the Kennedys, although Davis couldn't be sure that Bobby ever confided even in his own family. By that time Sinatra had been alienated from the Kennedys for a while, and Davis figured that none of them would have approved of Bobby dealing with Frank.

Peter Lawford told me he did know something was going on, but he never knew all the details. Sinatra had asked him to arrange a meeting with Bobby, and, after Lawford had done that, he never asked any questions.

When Bobby Kennedy stepped down from the post of attorney general, and the incumbent took over, a secret file containing the details Sinatra gave up was passed on, and in May 1965 a grand-jury investigation into interstate racketeering was launched. Sam Giancana was the prime target.

Sam the Cigar was no novice at this game. He made a deal of his own, and in return for promising to provide damning evidence against other mafiosi, he was granted immunity. He appeared in court in June, but despite the deal he'd made, at the last minute he refused to talk. It seemed that his peers had made it clear to

him that if he talked, he'd die. He was found in contempt of court
and sentenced to a term of one year in the Cook County Jail.

When Frank heard this, he allowed himself a big smile of self-
congratulation. He also later breathed a huge sigh of relief when
it became apparent that neither Giancana nor any of the other
racketeers ever discovered the part he had played in getting Sam
the Cigar into jail.

From time to time, the Summit – minus Peter Lawford and Joey
Bishop – still teamed up to perform in Las Vegas. Bobby
Kennedy went to see one of their shows, and there he met
Barbara Marx. She was a former showgirl, and the wife of Zeppo
Marx, one of the famous Marx Brothers. They lived next door to
Sinatra in Palm Springs.

Barbara, then in her thirties, was a stunning beauty, and it
wasn't long before she captured the attention of Bobby Kennedy
on the dance floor. Barbara was unhappy with her marriage to
Zeppo who, besides being much older than she was, spent much
of his time playing poker with his own friends on a boat he
owned in Acapulco. While he was away, Barbara liked to party.

For the next year, she was said to have enjoyed a secret affair with
Bobby Kennedy. Frank Sinatra frowned upon the affair because, as
Ava said, he already had his eyes on 'the long-legged Mrs Marx'.
Yet it would be more than ten years before Barbara Marx would
become the third and final Mrs Sinatra. It seems that, despite
Frank's secret pact with Bobby Kennedy, the affair between Bobby
and Barbara Marx cast a shadow over their agreement. It was not,
however, enough to stop Frank going ahead with his plans in
partnership with Kennedy to bring down Sam Giancana.

In 1997, Barbara Marx denied ever having been involved
romantically with Bobby Kennedy, saying in the *New York Post*
on 8 December, 'I was never that lucky. But I got even luckier
than that when I married Frank Sinatra in 1976.'

Chapter Fourteen

A Waiting Game

In 1965, Frank Sinatra flew off to Italy to make *Von Ryan's Express*. He was glad to be out of the United States for a while: he didn't want to be too available should Sam Giancana discover what he was up to.

The mid-sixties saw Sinatra in what Ava called 'a time of transition' – from the little tough guy 'in bed with the Mob and enjoying getting fucked by them' to the 'Chairman of the Board' who called the shots 'his way'. This was a description I recognised when I interviewed two of his co-stars from *Von Ryan's Express*, John Leyton (probably the first British actor to become a pop star) and James Brolin (who was then an up-and-coming contract player at Fox). Both painted vastly different pictures of Sinatra. Brolin told me:

'Sinatra was sort of at his prime. One day he would say, "Hello Jim, how are you today?" and the next you could say, "Hi, Frank," and he'd walk right by you. You never really knew where he was going to be at. I don't know if chemically he'd change from day to day or if his stars weren't right, or maybe that was the game that he played. If Brando plays games, at least he's consistent about it. You know if you run into Brando, he's gonna play mental chess with you, but if you run into Sinatra, you never know what the game is.'

When I later interviewed John Leyton, he said:

'When I first got out to Rome I was called the following day to the set where we were filming in a railway siding. I got there and hadn't even met the director Mark Robson until then. And he said, "Right, we're doing this scene", whatever it was, and it was a scene with Trevor Howard and Frank Sinatra.

'Mark Robson said, "Come over and meet Trevor and Frank," and I thought "This is ridiculous", and I pinched myself to see if I'd wake up. I was taken over and there was Trevor Howard standing to one side and there was Frank Sinatra standing in between two railway carriages, standing on one of the railway lines. And that's where I first met these two screen giants and played my first scene with them.

'Now, I'm sure that what Jim [Brolin] told you is absolutely true, and Sinatra could get bad tempered at times, but he never got bad tempered with me. I found Sinatra charming and I got on exceptionally well with him. I'm sure he was pretty nasty to other people in the film, but I can only judge him from my point of view. And from my point of view he was always very nice.

'It wasn't a very happy movie. Sinatra arrived and left in a helicopter with all his henchmen. It was "Frank Sinatra and Trevor Howard in ..." and there was Trevor Howard going out to the location in the car, bumping around in his old Citroën.

'We've been on the set since about eight o'clock and at about 10.30 nobody's shot anything. And then the helicopter arrives. Out steps Frank Sinatra; everybody's ready for him in front of the camera. Action! Camera! That's it! Cut! Print! He's back in the helicopter and back off home, and we're still standing there. So I think it's understandable if Trevor was put out by this favoured treatment Sinatra got.

'I've seen him get pretty bad tempered with people. In between shots, you want to sit and relax and not get hassled, but between shots he would sit down and there would be a ring of photographers round him going Click! Click! Click! Every now and then he would say, "Give me ten minutes, fellas," and they'd go away. But somebody would come back after seven minutes, and he'd be the one who gets slugged.

Ava was also in Italy, filming *The Bible ... In the Beginning* for John Huston. Word reached Frank that Ava had embarked on a tempestuous, and dangerous, affair with George Scott, who was playing Abraham to Ava's Sara. As Huston recalled:

'Scott is a man I do not like, although I think he is a wonderful actor. He claimed to be madly in love with Ava, and displayed jealousy that was, to say the least, in the extreme. When she didn't show him the attention he felt was due to him, he got very violent with her. He would drink heavily and literally lay into her.

'One night in the hotel where we were staying in Avenzzano, he got really very drunk and threatened Ava with actual physical violence. I leaped onto his back and wrapped my arms around his head so he couldn't see, and because the big bastard was so strong, he carried me around the bar on his back, trying to shake me off and bumping into tables and turning them over. But I'm a big bastard too! I hung on. Someone else persuaded Ava to leave the bar.'

When Sinatra heard how Scott had been treating Ava, he made a personal visit to the set and told Scott, in no uncertain terms, that if he laid another hand on Ava, he would personally kill him.

Ava remembered how, on the set, a couple of 'tough-looking guys' turned up and kept an eye on things. When they saw Scott getting rough with Ava, they moved in and threatened to break his kneecaps. 'I think John maybe found a couple of Mafia types and had them watch out for me, which was one time I was glad to see some hoods. God, I did love George because he could be so sweet and strong, but why I put up with what he did to me – well, I eventually put a stop to him.'

In her autobiography Ava said she thought it was Huston who

had hired the 'hoods', but Huston told me, 'I think Frank commissioned a couple of his guys to follow her and make sure he [Scott] behaved himself. But Scott was no gentleman.'

In fact, Ava admitted to me that Sinatra had made contact with someone who was probably an underboss of the Sicilian Mafia, able to do so because of his former friendship with Lucky Luciano, and the bodyguards were duly arranged.

In 1974, Huston admitted he never knew Sinatra very well. 'I admire him. He sticks by his guns and stands by his friends. Ava and he have a great affection for each other, and when she's in trouble, she always turns to him. I respect his kind of loyalty, regardless of what they say about him and his Mob connections. In fact, if the guys he had follow her around were from the Mob, then it's just as well he had those connections.'

It would seem that, even though he had largely shaken off the influence of the Mafia, there were still some friends in the Mob to whom Sinatra could turn. There may also have been some enemies who were keeping an eye on him. In 1965 Mia Farrow, who had begun dating Sinatra, had a frightening experience for which she was never able to find a full explanation.

She was driving home from Sinatra's Los Angeles apartment one night when she suddenly realised she was being followed by two men in a car. She tried to shake them off, but they hung onto her tail. She pulled into a gas station and ran to the phone to call Frank. Within minutes he was on the scene with a loaded gun, but there was no sign of the car that had been following her.

Sinatra seemed to have no explanation as to why anyone should follow, Mia, but it's almost certain that the men were either FBI agents tailing anyone who had anything to do with Sinatra, or men with more sinister motives. Either way, Frank decided that Mia should learn how to protect herself. He gave her a small pearl-handled gun and taught her to use it. She was reluctant to carry a gun, and proved such an awful shot that even

Frank agreed she ought not to carry it after all.

Frank played out a nervous waiting game throughout 1965. He wanted to keep himself busy while Sam Giancana sweated out his time in Cook County Jail. There was no knowing as yet if his plan to aid the FBI would reach the ears of the incarcerated Giancana, and to ease the waiting he kept busy with movies. He also made a concert tour of six cities, featuring the Count Basie Band – his first tour with a band in twenty years. That year also saw the release of the *Sinatra '65* album, which was a compilation of some of his best songs of the previous five years. Then he did another album, *Moonlight*.

Sinatra began 1966 by playing the Sands, again with Basie. The shows were recorded for release later in the year as a live album, *Sinatra at the Sands*. That was also the year when Frank married Mia – and Pat Lawford divorced Peter.

Mia seemed not to come into contact with anyone she recognised as being a part of the Mob, but she did recall how she would find herself in Las Vegas 'sitting with the hookers as I had so many times', while Frank and other men told jokes and laughed. There was always a part of Sinatra that didn't need women as constant companions. He liked to have the company of men who enjoyed the same lifestyle he had. And he certainly enjoyed having the company of men who treated him like a king and laughed at all his jokes.

Not too surprisingly, the marriage lasted just two years.

Sinatra felt immediately uneasy when he learned that Sam Giancana had been released after his year of incarceration. He was particularly anxious when he got a call from Giancana, announcing that he was free and looking forward to seeing his entertainer friend.

Determined to avoid any contact with Giancana, Sinatra made his excuses for being unable to meet with him.

'What the fuck is this?' asked Giancana. 'You can't spare five minutes to see a pal who's been locked up for a year?'

'I got commitments,' Frank told him. 'We'll get together as soon as I'm able.'

'Who the fuck do you think you're talking to? Ain't I the guy who got you fucking jobs when nobody wanted you? Ain't I the guy who set you up at the Cal-Neva?'

Frank got frustrated and said, 'Yeah, and you're the guy who lost me my fucking gaming licence. And you're the guy who sent me the skinned head of a lamb – twice.'

If this sounded like mad talk from someone who was speaking to a seasoned killer, it probably was. Yet Frank knew that by then Giancana had lost a great deal of his power. Others had taken control of the rackets in Chicago, and Giancana was considered something of a liability now that the Justice Department had him by the tail.

'I can make sure you're as dead as that fucking lamb,' Giancana ranted.

'Not if I make sure you're fucking dead first.'

Those were probably the last words Sinatra ever spoke to Sam Giancana.

Taking no chances, Sinatra got in touch with someone 'he trusted at the Bureau', as Ava put it, to find out what they were doing about Giancana. It turned out that someone at the CIA had 'pulled strings' with the Justice Department to prevent Giancana from further prosecution. They wanted to protect him.

Sinatra was understandably uneasy, but with Bobby Kennedy no longer attorney general, he had no real ally who could pursue convictions against Giancana. So he pulled his trump card. He told whoever it was he was talking to at the FBI that he was prepared to go public once and for all in regard to what really happened to Marilyn Monroe – even if it meant dragging the Kennedy name into it.

He was told that it would be a bad idea to do that. Bobby had decided the time was not right to bring Giancana and the others involved in the JFK assassination to justice. Frank, however, was determined that he would not let Giancana get away with the murder of Monroe. He told the FBI agent, 'As long as Giancana is free, he won't be safe.'

'What do you mean?'

'Just that.'

Concerning Frank's threat on Giancana's life, Ava said that she felt he was just blowing off steam and thinking off the top of his head. Ava, as far as she could tell, was the only one to whom he confided this story. Not even Sammy Davis had heard about that. Davis wasn't surprised, though. 'I know a lot of people say Frank don't got principles. But when it really matters, he's full of 'em. So if he did have it in mind to have Giancana killed, okay, so it's not legal, but it's the way Giancana dealt with things.'

Ava was relieved that Frank didn't have to carry out his threat. 'I know Frank broke plenty of laws just being in partnership with those fucking hoods,' she said, 'but to actually murder even a goddamn killer like that fucking Giancana would have been too much. That would have been the end of Frank's career for good.'

She told him as much, too.

The threat on Giancana's life by Sinatra did not come to fruition. The CIA saw to that. It may well be that word reached them that Sinatra – or someone – was prepared to put a contract on Giancana's life, and they prudently decided that Giancana would be safest and would serve them best if he were out of the country. So they sent him into exile in Mexico. Frank was convinced that his actions were behind Giancana's Mexican sojourn.

Sinatra's plan was one of the best-kept secrets, even in the entertainment business, where secrets are almost impossible to keep. Eddie Fisher noted that Sam was 'permitted to retire to

Mexico' because he had made the mistake of 'enjoying life too much' and was 'the subject of too much publicity'.

Giancana's exile was in part a punishment brought about by Sinatra's actions, but it certainly suited the CIA's purposes to have him in Mexico. From there, through contacts like Johnny Roselli and those still loyal to him in the Outfit, Giancana could help them take care of certain matters. He would be able to carry out CIA operations in Latin America, he would be free to work with associates in Europe and the Middle East; he could control drug-trafficking in Asia; and he could provide a certain amount of assistance to agents in Vietnam.

Oblivious to all this, Eddie Fisher met up with Giancana while he was working in Mexico. It seems that by this time Fisher had taken Sinatra's favoured place in Giancana's life. 'I loved him like a brother,' wrote Fisher, who also said that he was 'in awe of him'. While Fisher was working in Mexico City, Giancana stayed with him for three weeks, sleeping in a small room in Eddie's hotel suite. Giancana told Fisher, 'You don't answer the phone, don't answer the door. I'll take care of everything.' Fisher realised that Giancana was in constant danger.

It was around this time that Frank ran into his old nemesis in the Mob, Johnny Roselli. I don't know for sure where this reunion took place, but it was on Sinatra's own ground – possibly his Hollywood home – and he was certainly surrounded by his bodyguards. For some reason, however, Sinatra agreed to see Roselli alone, without the bodyguards in the room.

Roselli had been away from Hollywood for the past few years, living and working in Florida in close partnership with one of Giancana's most trusted cohorts, Santo Trafficante. Sinatra was cautious, not knowing if Roselli was there to check him out and report back to Giancana, or if he had another agenda.

Considering his hatred for Roselli, Sinatra was courteous, offering him a drink and making him feel welcome. Roselli made small talk about Sam's travels and how he had been to Rome for a private audience with Pope Paul. Sinatra listened with feigned interest, and finally decided it was time to come to the point. He asked Roselli what he wanted.

Roselli said it wasn't about what he wanted, but about what Sam wanted. He said that Chicago's interests in Hollywood had been largely forgotten with him in Florida and Sam in Mexico. Giancana had sent him to see Sinatra, to ask if Sam could still count on him.

Sinatra wisely pointed out that he was under constant surveillance by the FBI and was in no position to do anything apart from concentrate on his career. He suggested that it was possible that this sudden visit by Roselli may not have gone unnoticed. This riled Roselli, who began to remind Frank of all the favours Sam had done for him. Ordinarily, Frank would have lost his temper at this point, but he kept his cool, and explained how sorry he was not to be able to help his old friend out at this time. He promised that he would not forget 'everything Sam's done' – and he meant it, though not in the way he wanted Roselli to understand – and he suggested that he call on him again at a later date when, he hoped, things would have 'cooled off'.

He could see that Roselli was mad, and he guessed that Johnny might well have wanted to take a slug at him, but Roselli knew there were bodyguards nearby, and he made a smiling tactical retreat.

The two men shook hands, and Frank told Roselli to send Sam his best wishes, and then he had one of his bodyguards accompany Roselli off the premises.

Frank was relieved when Roselli had gone, and he wondered if there would be any unfortunate ramifications to follow. He never did know for sure if Roselli had been there to ask a real favour on behalf of Giancana, or if he'd been sent to test him.

The FBI were frustrated because they were unable to lay a

hand on Sam in Mexico, but exile for Giancana suited Frank just fine. He knew, however, that he would have to be careful where he travelled in the future. Giancana had a long arm, and it stretched far around the globe. Frank felt he had done all he could to put Giancana out of harm's way, and he knew that, despite the power base Sam would be able to build in Mexico, it was a definite comedown for the man who once ran Chicago and much of America.

That situation also suited Bobby Kennedy, who contacted Sinatra when he heard that Frank seemed determined to make Giancana pay with his life. 'I didn't like the idea of you dragging me into your vendetta over Marilyn,' he told Frank, 'but remember this. When the time comes, when I'm president, you have a friend, and together we'll bring Giancana and all those who killed Jack to heel. But remember, this is just between you and me. Otherwise we don't stand a chance.'

Sinatra agreed, and looked forward to proving his patriotism when the time came to work hand in hand with Bobby Kennedy and finally clean up the corruption that lay in the dark corners of the American government.

Sinatra continued to be busy making movies. Just before *Robin and the Seven Hoods*, he had starred with Dean Martin, Anita Ekberg and Ursula Andress in the 1963 comedy Western *Four for Texas*. Robert Aldrich, a man who could be as gentle as he was tough, had directed that film. When I interviewed Aldrich, I asked him if he had found Sinatra a difficult man to direct, considering the reputation he had gained during the fifties with what I called his 'Mob-style tactics'. Aldrich told me:

'I think it would be true to say that Frank had not completely given up those so-called Mob-style tactics. But this was *my* film, which *I* produced, and I made a point of telling Frank that. He said to me, "You're the boss."'

'But it was never quite that cut and dried when directing Frank Sinatra. He's a complex kind of actor. For much of the time it was easy, because he would arrive on the set when we were all ready for him, and he didn't need to rehearse much, and neither did Dean [Martin]. They just bounced off each other, and that made it very easy. But it had its difficult moments, like when we'd finish a take and I'd say, "Let's do that one again", because there was something in the scene that I didn't like. Frank would say, "Did I fuck up?" and I'd say, "No, it wasn't you, Frank," and he'd say, "Then let's move on." So he tried to throw his weight around in that way because he felt if what he did was right, there was no need to reshoot. I think he was afraid he wouldn't catch that moment again.

'One day I asked him why he was like that, and he said, "When I was in *Guys and Dolls*, Marlon [Brando] would want to rehearse a scene over and over because he came from that fucking Method school of acting." But Frank was purely an instinctive actor, and if he got it right the first time, he didn't have the confidence to get it right a second time. So he told the director on that picture, Joe [Mankiewicz], to let him know when Marlon had finished rehearsing, and he'd come and do his shot.

'I tried to tell Frank that he had all the talent he needed to get it right as many times as it took, but he insisted he didn't need to do it more than once. That's simplifying it, because there were times when he did blow his lines, and then he and Dean would fall about in fits of laughter, so there were plenty of light moments on the set. But he could create tension, too. And he could have done it all a lot better. It was, perhaps, too casual a performance. Too *Frank Sinatra*! But that's what he wanted to be in the film, just Frank Sinatra, and I made the mistake of settling for that. He could have been so much better, and so could the film. It was too much like a Rat Pack picture. But I don't blame actors for my failures. There are times, however, when a director can only make the best of the tools he's got.

'The one thing you didn't mention to him is anything that might relate to the Mafia. I didn't care too much what the deal was between him and any hoods, just so long as he did the job we were paying him to do. I found that out one day when someone on the set accused him of playing the tough guy with too many friends in low places. He exploded and said, "If you're referring to what I think you're referring to, you're dead wrong, and one day I'm gonna fucking prove it." I don't know what he meant by that, but you know and I know and we all know he was in with that low life. But I got the feeling that when we worked together, he was really trying to put it all behind him.'

Right after *Robin and the Seven Hoods* released in 1964, Sinatra went straight into *Marriage on the Rocks*, a subject he knew much about, which he produced for Warners. Dean Martin co-starred again, and there was also a part for Frank's daughter, Nancy. He then produced and starred in *Assault on a Queen*, released in 1966, having also done a favour to Kirk Douglas and Melville Shavelson by guest-starring in their epic *Cast a Giant Shadow* (1966), filmed in Israel.

Sinatra was back in the US for *The Naked Runner*, which he didn't produce, but his friend Brad Dexter did. It was a success in 1967 after a run of mediocre flops. Then, in quick succession, he did two private-eye thrillers, *Tony Rome* and *The Detective* in 1967 followed with *Lady in Cement* in 1968. After a break of two years he did the terrible *Dirty Dingus McGee*, then suddenly he seemed to lose interest in movies.

By then, however, a new tragedy had struck America.

Chapter Fifteen

The Kiss of Death

Bobby Kennedy had been busy running for president – as well as trying to track down the tapes that connected him to Marilyn Monroe. At some point, probably early in 1968, Bobby and Frank had a secret meeting, and Kennedy revealed the progress he had made.

Before Marilyn died, Bobby had discovered that a wire-tap expert, Bernie Spindel, had been the man who had wired Peter Lawford's home on the orders of Jimmy Hoffa – who had acted on the orders of Sam Giancana. Bobby had personally met with Spindel in a car, sometime in 1966, and had tried in vain to persuade him to hand over the tapes, offering him as much as 25,000 dollars for them. Spindel obviously felt they were worth a lot more and declined the offer, so Bobby ordered Manhattan's District Attorney Frank Hogan to raid Spindel's New York home and seize all tapes and equipment as evidence of illegal wire-tapping.

Spindel sued in the New York Supreme Court for the return of the tapes, and said in an affidavit that among the tapes was 'evidence concerning the circumstances surrounding the cause of death of Marilyn Monroe, which strongly suggest that the officially reported circumstances of her demise were erroneous'.

Among the tapes were conversations picked up from a bug he'd
planted on Marilyn's phone.

Nevertheless, Spindel went to prison, while a careless member
of the DA's staff told a newspaper reporter that 'the tapes
indicated Marilyn was murdered and that somehow Bobby was
involved if only as a catalyst causing someone else to do it'. This
remark, which was published, has led those who favour the
theory that Bobby Kennedy had her killed to believe they were
right. In fact, those theorists suggest, rightly, that Bobby's
dumping Marilyn and then being at Marilyn's home on the day
she died was a precursor to her murder, by 'someone else'.

Then the tapes managed to disappear.

Bobby reported to Sinatra that he had hired a private detective
to find Spindel's tapes. They turned up in the possession of a
policeman who wanted 50,000 dollars for them. A deal was made
for the tapes to be handed over to a group of Republicans.

Bobby also reported that the FBI were keeping a close
surveillance on Sam Giancana as he moved throughout Mexico, and
then into South America. Bobby told Sinatra he was determined to
bring Giancana back to the United States to face charges for his
crimes. He was even willing to risk exposing his affair with Monroe
to do so, and he asked Frank for his help and advice.

Sinatra agreed to co-operate in every way. In return Kennedy
would do all he could to help Sinatra regain his gaming licence.
Two FBI agents trusted by Kennedy were assigned to work
secretly with Sinatra.

What Sinatra did not offer to do for Bobby Kennedy was to do
what he had done for his brother Jack, and that was to campaign
for him. The truth was, Sinatra did not support Bobby's bid for
the presidency. In fact, he had planned to support Vice President
Hubert Humphrey. One would have thought that, given the secret
pact Sinatra had made with Kennedy, he would have been behind
Bobby, but the truth of the matter was that he had mixed

emotions about Jack's brother. Frank was never sure if Bobby had dissuaded JFK from staying at his Palm Springs home because of his Mob links, and he had certainly never felt the same close association with Bobby that he had enjoyed with Jack. On the other hand, during the time of Frank Jr's abduction, Bobby had been there for him. Now they were there for each other, to solve a shared problem – that is, Sam Giancana.

Frank met with the two agents Kennedy assigned to him and he began to give them details about Giancana that even the FBI didn't know. It was agreed that Sinatra would never have to testify, which meant that all the information he gave them would still have to be proven, but it nevertheless gave the agents leads that they could follow up without implicating Frank in any way. Their sole concern was to get Sam Giancana, and Sinatra was giving them the tools to accomplish that feat.

Sinatra knew, through his own connections, where Giancana was most likely to be found in Mexico – in Cuernavaca, where Giancana lived in a luxurious house. The problem was, CIA agents were doing their best to protect Giancana. The FBI decided to give details of Giancana's life in Mexico to a reporter for *Life* magazine, Sandy Smith, who wrote an exposé on Giancana's life in crime and described how he was now living in a comfortable residence in Mexico outside American jurisdiction.

Sinatra knew he was playing with fire, but he was determined to destroy Giancana's empire. Since his first secret meeting with Bobby Kennedy, he had been able to supply the FBI with information that allowed them to indict no fewer than twenty-four members of the Outfit in 1967. As far as Frank knew, neither Giancana nor any of the Outfit ever suspected his part in their downfall. If they had, he would not have lived into old age.

When Ava learned of all this, she 'aged ten years', as she put it. Ava was his confidante, and she began to wish that she wasn't. Frank told her, 'Trust me. The FBI are on my side now, and I'm on theirs. I'm doing this for my country, for Marilyn and for President Kennedy.'

Ava replied, 'I hope the CIA see it that way.'

'They'll never know.'

There were many nights when Ava lay awake, worrying what might happen to Frank.

Sinatra and Kennedy had agreed to meet again sometime in the future. The future, however, was cut short. Robert Kennedy was assassinated on 4 June 1968. That was the very day on which the tapes of Bobby and Marilyn were to be handed over to the Republicans. With Bobby dead, the tapes were no longer needed, and they were never collected. The whereabouts of those tapes are no longer known.

Sammy Davis recalled that many of those who, like him, were liberals had spoken out against the Vietnam War and blamed President Lyndon B Johnson (who succeeded JFK) not only for sending American troops to Vietnam, but also for not getting the war won when he committed America to the conflict. But Frank, a legendary liberal, had been conspicuous by his silence when it came to condemning the war and the administration that had fuelled it. Davis said that Sinatra had not spoken out against the war simply because he was a patriot and did not want to embarrass the American president, whoever he was. To condemn the president was, to Frank, the same as condemning the country.

Johnson was certainly not the liberals' choice, therefore, and Davis felt that the vice president seemed hardly likely to gain the support of Sinatra. Yet Frank was prepared to back Humphrey, mainly because he just did not want Bobby Kennedy to become president. It really had nothing to do with politics: it was a personal thing, pure and simple. And yet, said Davis, he had the feeling that in May 1968 Frank – who by then was openly supporting Humphrey – might well have been having a change of heart, and that would have been due to the secret pact Frank and

Bobby had made. With Bobby's life cut short, however, nobody would ever know for sure which way Sinatra would have gone. As it was, he continued to support Humphrey – but Frank's past was catching up with him.

Not long after Bobby's assassination, Sinatra was incensed to learn about a botched FBI operation launched in an attempt to lure Giancana out of Mexico. The home of Giancana's daughter Bonnie and her husband Tony Tisci in Tucson, Arizona, was attacked by gunmen. Bullets tore through the windows into the front room, and it was a miracle that no one was killed. Shortly after, there was a similar attack at the Tucson home of the New York crime lord Joe Bonanno. When news reached Frank that this was part of an FBI operation, he contacted the agents assigned to him and asked them what the hell they were doing attacking the home of Giancana's daughter, whose only crime was to have a gangster for a father.

Frank was told that they had personally had nothing to do with the operation and that it was the brainchild of some agent in Tucson who had hired three local gangsters to launch the attacks. The FBI were embarrassed by the whole thing, especially as it failed to bring Giancana out of Mexico, and they were trying to keep the truth under wraps.

When Sinatra was told that the operation was launched only as a means of trying to lay hands on Sam Giancana, Frank told them, 'You want your hands on Sam, *I'll* help you get your hands on Sam. I told you I will. But you don't go shooting up innocent people to do it.'

Sinatra's secret promises to the FBI did nothing to counteract the continuing allegations made against him. Joseph L Nellis, who had questioned Sinatra privately at the time of the Kefauver hearings, wrote to Humphrey about Sinatra's Mob connections and warned him that, by allowing Sinatra to support him, he might well be getting 'support from the underworld'.

Nellis would not have known of Sinatra's vendetta and of his rejection of the Mafia, and it is doubtful that Frank let Humphrey in on the fact. Nevertheless, Humphrey did not, at that point, cut Sinatra off completely. Then Martin McNamara, former Assistant US Attorney in Washington, who was also ignorant of Sinatra's secret intentions and actions, told Henry Peterson, head of the Justice Department's organised-crime division, that Sinatra still had debts to pay to the likes of Sam Giancana and Skinny D'Amato.

Neither McNamara nor Peterson, who in turn warned Humphrey, was able to provide any solid evidence against Sinatra. It may be that a certain small faction of the FBI who were in on the pact that Frank had made with Bobby were not about to break Sinatra's cover by letting McNamara, Peterson or Humphrey know what Frank was actually doing for them. In consequence, Humphrey suddenly refused to take Sinatra's calls.

That didn't stop Frank from continuing to support Humphrey and, according to Sammy Davis, Frank was actually sending a message which told them 'to go screw themselves because he was still going to support him [Humphrey] whether he liked it or not'. Davis said that Frank had worked hard for Humphrey before suddenly finding himself out in the cold. He'd given him tips about public relations and how to use make-up for television appearances, and he even paid for advertisements in the press declaring his support for Humphrey.

This time, however, not even Frank Sinatra could help win his chosen man the presidency, as he had done for JFK. In fact, said Davis, Frank began to wonder if he was, by now, 'the kiss of death' for any presidential candidate. The presidency went to Richard Nixon.

Frank Sinatra didn't care any more. He wanted only to make sure that Sam Giancana paid for the death of Marilyn Monroe and then to get on with his life, which he was gradually turning around.

Giancana could not be lured out of Mexico, and throughout 1968 and 1969 he kept on the move through South and Central America. He also managed to travel abroad to Europe, and particularly throughout the Middle East, proving very useful to various CIA operations.

Sometime around 1969, Sinatra's FBI agents told him that they could not locate Giancana, who had left his old residence and taken up a new one – but they didn't know where. They asked him if he could help.

Frank arranged a meeting with Johnny Roselli. They had not met or spoken since Roselli had come to Hollywood to ask Sinatra to do some favours for Giancana. Frank told Roselli that he felt he was now in a better position to help Giancana, but he wanted to meet with Sam face to face. He asked Roselli if he could arrange it.

Roselli told him that Sam didn't dare set foot outside Mexico for fear of being immediately apprehended by the FBI. So Frank asked if he could go to Mexico to meet with Sam. Roselli said he would arrange for Frank to meet Sam at his estate in San Cristobel.

Frank was able to report to his agents the town where Giancana now lived, but he didn't relish the prospect of having to make the journey to Mexico to meet with Sam purely for the purpose of maintaining his cover story. Then, by an ironic stroke of fate, his dark past caught up with him again and provided him with the prefect excuse for being unable to meet with Giancana. He was called before the New Jersey State Commission on Investigation in February 1970, to answer questions under oath. It was one more cross Sinatra had to bear because of his past associations, and he continued to maintain his ignorance regarding organised crime. In fact, in retaliation for the subpoena, he filed a lawsuit in federal court in a vain attempt to halt the proceedings.

'I do not have any knowledge of the extent to which organised crime functions in the state of New Jersey, or whether there is such a thing as organised crime,' he wrote in his statement.

It was a blatant lie, and he must have wished he could go public with his undercover activities in regard to his work with a section of the FBI to bring Giancana to heel. He had, of course, no option but to stay silent on the matter.

His attorney, Mickey Rudin, managed to get the commission to allow Frank a secret session in which he agreed to be questioned under oath. Yet even under oath, he swore that he had never been aware that Sam Giancana was connected to the Mafia, and he maintained that he did not know about Luciano's reputation as a Mafia boss.

He was finally asked, 'Do you know anyone who's a member of the Mob?'

He flatly replied, 'No, sir.'

'Do you know anyone who's a member of any organisation that would come under the category of organised crime?'

'No, sir.'

Afterwards he complained, 'I'm tired of being considered an authority on organised crime. For many years, every time some Italian names are involved in any inquiry, I get a subpoena. I appear, I am asked questions about scores of persons unknown to me based on rumours and events which have never happened. Then I am subjected to the type of publicity I do not desire and do not seek.'

When Ava Gardner heard all this, she contacted Frank and again reminded him of the dangers he had brought upon himself. He told her that he wished he could just admit that he did know who Sam Giancana really was and get it out in the open, but that would simply have led to unending questioning on the subject. It would probably end his career, and it would also prevent him from carrying out his vendetta.

It was his vendetta, perhaps more than the fear of damage to his career, that forced Sinatra to maintain his stance of ignorance about such people as Giancana. It was his ongoing denial about organised crime, despite the evidence to the contrary, that resulted in the many allegations, rumours and opinions offered up by so many that lasted the rest of his life. Some saw his denials as pure arrogance. What no one seemed to question was why the FBI, who clearly had evidence against him, didn't simply supply the New Jersey State Commission on Investigation with that evidence. The reason was simple: Siantra had friends in the FBI and he was, at that time, still forging his links with those agents to whom Bobby Kennedy had introduced him.

Sinatra knew – and he told Ava as much – that he was being protected, but it was not the end of his current problems. In Las Vegas in September 1970, one of his own employees cashed in 75,000 dollars of chips so Sinatra could play blackjack, and this fact came to the attention of the IRS, who had an undercover agent investigating the relationship between the entertainment business and the underworld.

The IRS agent discovered that Sinatra had IOUs at a number of casinos for large amounts of money which he'd lost gambling. Yet the IOUs were rarely, if ever, deducted from the salaries he commanded for performing at the clubs.

At Caesar's Palace, an argument broke out between Sinatra and the manager, Sanford Waterman, over Sinatra's IOU, ending with Waterman producing a gun and aiming it at Frank. Sinatra was heard to say, 'I hope you like that gun, because you may have to eat it.'

Since this happened in front of witnesses at the blackjack table, the story got into the press. Faced with a report supplied by the IRS agent on top of all the newspaper reports, the local District

Attorney George Franklin decided he would personally question
Sinatra. He said he would be asking Sinatra 'about who owned
the nightclubs where he sang, the early days, who started him on
his way, and his friendships with the underworld'.

The version of events that emerged from the DA's office was,
as Sinatra put it, 'straight out of a comic strip'. The DA said that
as Sinatra walked away from Waterman, he said, 'The Mob will
take care of you.' He also claimed that Waterman 'still had
fingermarks on his throat where Sinatra grabbed him'.

To fend off any interrogation by the DA, Sinatra offered his own
version of events to the newspapers. He said he'd only just sat
down at the blackjack table and hadn't even placed a bet when
Waterman came over and told the dealer, 'Don't deal to this man.'

Sinatra said he got up and told Waterman, 'Put your name on
the marquee and I'll come to see what kind of business you do.'
Then he just walked away. 'As for his injuries,' Sinatra told the
press, 'I never touched him.'

The DA had to concede there was no case to answer, and there
is some indication that once more certain FBI agents were
protecting Sinatra.

It didn't end there, however. In July 1972 Sinatra was served
with yet another subpoena, this time to appear before the House
Select Committee on Crime. This committee had been
investigating the links between organised crime and sport.
Sinatra again complained, saying, 'It's always something, always
some goddamn investigation, and I'm in the middle of it.'

This time it was about an investment Sinatra had made ten
years earlier in Berkshire Downs in Hancock, Massachusetts.
Other investors were the New England Mafia boss Raymond
Patricia – who in 1972 was serving ten years in the Atlanta
Penitentiary for conspiracy to murder – and Tommy Lucchese of
the New York Mob.

At the hearing on 18 July, a published article was given in

evidence with the headline, 'Witness links Sinatra with reputed Mafia figure'. In the article, Joseph 'the Baron' Barboza, an enforcer for the Mafia, said that Sinatra had provided a business front for Raymond Patricia. Sinatra was incensed and said, 'That's charming. This bum went running off at the mouth, and I resent it. I won't have it. I am not a second-class citizen. Let's get this straightened out.'

He made sure it got straightened out by handing over a file to the FBI that detailed his involvement in Berkshire Downs, showing that he had returned his investment profits upon learning the identity of his partners. For once, Sinatra had told the truth.

During questioning, he was asked about Tommy Lucchese, and he answered that he had met Lucchese a few times while he was performing at the 500 Club in Atlantic City. When asked if he knew that Lucchese was a gangster, Sinatra simply replied, 'That's his problem, not mine. Let's dispense with that kind of question.'

Again, he was being protected, and it didn't take long for agents to produce the incarcerated Raymond Patricia, who told the commission that he had never met Frank Sinatra.

That protection paid off, because Frank was able to provide more information, which led the FBI to launch a covert operation to cause trouble within the ranks of the Chicago Outfit. Sinatra knew the right people in the Outfit who had certain grudges, and the FBI were able to employ them to create a sense of gangland warfare. This resulted in the contract killing of Richard Cain, Giancana's right-hand man in Chicago, in 1973.

Through it all, the agents with whom Sinatra worked maintained his anonymity. This was by no means a painless task for Sinatra, who could, after all, have wiped his slate clean by allowing his name to come out as one who was aiding the FBI. There was really no option, however. To have done so would have put his life in jeopardy, and also his career, and that was not a gamble he was prepared to take. His only reward would be the eventual downfall of Sam Giancana.

By 1974, Giancana's health was deteriorating and he was unable to travel extensively, so he remained in his walled home at San Cristobel. Sinatra, who had been instrumental in helping to locate Mooney's whereabouts in Mexico, was told that a mission was being planned to kidnap Giancana – who, over the years, had won the favour of the Mexican government and even the president. The operation was completely covert.

It happened very suddenly in July 1974. Giancana was suddenly ambushed and literally kidnapped by four immigration agents and taken to Mexico City. From there he was flown to Texas, where the FBI met him in San Antonio. He was immediately served with a subpoena to appear before a Chicago grand jury.

One night Eddie Fisher received a call from the comedian Guy Marx, who told him, 'You gotta come for dinner tonight because Sheila's going to be there.'

Fisher knew that 'Sheila' was just another alias for Sam Giancana. When Fisher arrived at the restaurant, he saw Giancana sitting with his back to the window. Knowing that this was hardly the safest position for a gangster, Fisher asked him, 'How come you're sitting with your back to the window?'

'Eddie, you're going up to Vegas to do your show, and I'm going up to Washington to do my show.'

That was the last time Fisher ever saw Sam Giancana.

It finally looked like the end of the road for Giancana – and Frank Sinatra felt very satisfied that at long last he had paid Giancana back for all he had done. His vendetta had finally been completed.

Chapter Sixteen

Secrets Revealed

It was in 1969 that I first met Ava Gardner. I was just a messenger boy, aged seventeen, for Cinerama, delivering a package on behalf of my managing director who was an old friend of Ava.

She had recently moved to London, to a flat in Enismore Gardens, and I found myself so badly in need of the lavatory that I had the audacity to ask if I could avail myself of her facilities. It was a heady feeling for a young film fan like myself to find himself in Ava Gardner's bathroom!

All I can say is, she took an immediate shine to me, and before long we were having clandestine meetings at a Knightsbridge hotel. Why she preferred to meet away from her home, I don't know, but when a Hollywood queen invites you to spend nights with her at a place of her choosing, you tend not to say no.

A lot of what I learned at that time was 'pillow talk', which I generated purely through my insistence on asking questions about Hollywood, movies, Frank Sinatra and other stars she'd known and loved. It came to an end when I fell into a serious relationship with a girl my own age and got married in 1973.

Ava made numerous attempts to seduce me even then, and when I turned her down, she asked, 'Why not?'

'Because I'm married,' I told her.

'What has that got to do with anything?'

Fortunately, it did not put an end to our friendship, and I continued making visits to her home, where I learned to drink Scotch and she would sometimes cook me steak.

I don't know what it was about me that made Ava take such a shine to me. In those days I had a naive fascination for movies and movie stars. There must have been a certain charm about me, because there were a number of my betters for whom I worked who wanted to take me under their parental wings. To them, I seemed to be the son they never had.

I think part of the attraction Ava had for me lay in my intense enthusiasm and knowledge of films – but my knowledge was sadly limited. The first day I met her she mentioned Frank Sinatra, and I responded with some awe, '*You* know Frank *Sinatra*?'

She threw her head back, gave a loud, throaty laugh and said, 'My God, there's a whole generation out there who know nothing about me.'

I tried to stammer an apology for my ignorance, but she said, 'It's okay. It's very sobering to know I'm not the centre of the world.'

In 1974 I worked briefly for John Huston, who was in London working on pre-production for *The Man who Would Be King*. I'd met Huston a couple of years before when he was in the UK to make *The Macintosh Man*, and I was learning from him how to write screenplays. My ambition in those days was to be a film director and, with no film schools in existence, I was learning the trade any way I could. He felt I should follow his example and become a screenwriter first.

When I learned he was staying at the Connaught Hotel in London in 1974, I contacted him and asked if I could basically become his dogsbody for a week, just to continue learning. I was working at Columbia then, in the publicity department, and since he had a deal with Columbia to distribute *The Man who Would Be*

King, he seemed amenable to my proposition. Every evening for a week, and some afternoons when I could escape from the Columbia office in Wardour Street, I was in his company soaking up everything I could.

One time the subject of Ava came up, and Huston told me how he had once tried to seduce her in her swimming pool through hypnotism, but had failed miserably. Then he said to me, 'Has she taken you to bed yet?'

For some reason I panicked and lied. 'No,' I said.

He said, 'You do surprise me,' as though he saw through my lie.

We arranged to see Ava one day, and it was on that day that the conversation arose about Marilyn Monroe's death. That's when Ava decided, for reasons of her own which I never fully understood, that I should know everything.

Not only did I learn that there were many in Hollywood who didn't believe that Monroe had killed herself, Huston among them, but both Huston and I were given an account of a visit to Ava's home by Peter Lawford in 1969.

He had turned up drunk at her house and confessed his part in the cover-up of Marilyn's death. Ava already knew many of the facts, but this was the first time her old friend Lawford had told her himself.

His confession had been sparked by a phone call he had received following the assassination of Bobby Kennedy. He was told, 'First it was Monroe. Then the president. And now we've dealt with Bobby. Just so you know, if you decide to open your fucking mouth about what you know, you'll be next.'

He was in fear for his life, and he was also racked with guilt over the death of Marilyn – as he was to be for the rest of his life. He felt, for whatever reason – probably just a case of friendship, and the fact that Ava now lived away from Hollywood – that Ava was the one person in whom he could confide. Just as Sinatra had always done.

That phone call Lawford had received had finally put a great deal into perspective for him. He knew for sure now that the deaths of Monroe, JFK and Bobby Kennedy were linked, and that all three killings were handled by assassins from the same organisation – or organisations. What he didn't know were many of the details about Sinatra's secret dealings with Bobby Kennedy to expose the truth behind the murders of Marilyn and the president – but he learned about them that day from Ava.

Lawford may have been drunk, but when he began to understand that he was in the deep end simply because of what he had come to realise – that Sam Giancana had indeed been the brains behind the murder of Monroe – he began to sober up. It didn't take a genius to figure out that Giancana had been in collaboration with the CIA, and that both groups had maintained their alliance, through Sam Giancana, to take out John Kennedy and then Bobby.

Ava advised Lawford to do as he'd been told and keep his mouth shut, as he wailed and cried over what he perceived to be his own guilt. He knew that by protecting Bobby Kennedy on the day Marilyn died, he'd fallen into the hands of the assassins. Ava told him that Bobby had only himself to blame and that nobody, certainly not Peter, could have prevented the tragic series of events that had begun in 1962 and ended in 1968.

She didn't see or hear from Lawford again until 1974. By then she had told Huston and me the story Peter had told her five years earlier. It just so happened that around that time I was trying to get into journalism, although I didn't tell Ava because she was paranoid about 'goddamn reporters'. (When I finally became a full-time staff writer for *Film Review* magazine, she said, 'What the fucking hell do you wanna be a goddam reporter for? Be an actor, for God's sake.' It became my main motivation to become an actor.) One of my first attempts at journalism was to interview Peter Lawford, who came to London in 1974 to promote *That's*

Entertainment. It was in that formal setting that Lawford gave me his 'official' version of events regarding his falling-out with Frank Sinatra, as well as Marilyn Monroe's 'suicide.'

Shortly after that interview, which Ava knew nothing about, she decided to get Lawford and me up to her flat, and in no uncertain terms told Lawford to give me the true tale of events. He was pretty much out of his head with whatever he'd been drinking or sniffing, and gave no sign of remembering me or recognising me from our interview. It was as though we were meeting for the first time, and I saw no reason to remind him of our previous encounter.

He asked Ava why he should tell me anything and Ava told him, 'Because this is the generation who has to know. We'll all be dead and gone one day, and they'll bury the fucking truth with us all.'

She kept him well stocked with strong coffee as she prompted him to relate his story. Much of the time he seemed unable to get the words out, so Ava related the events as she recalled them, and he either nodded confirmation or corrected her in a slurred voice.

When the session was at an end, he begged me to keep it hushed up. Here was a man who looked a complete wreck, behaved like one, and was still in fear for his life. Whether it was the drink or the drugs talking, however, he took enough of a liking to me to invite me to a party he was throwing that evening. Ava became very defensive about me, and recommended that I didn't go, but, when Lawford said that Sammy Davis Jr would be there, she ceased her objections. Then, without my knowing, she gave Davis a call, asking him to make sure I didn't get led down the same path Peter trod.

When I arrived at the Mayfair house where the party was being held, I recognised a number of celebrities and discovered there were also some politicians present, whom I didn't recognise. There were plenty of high-class hookers.

Lawford introduced me to Sammy Davis, although he couldn't remember my name – only that he had met me at Ava's flat. Davis knew immediately who I was, having received Ava's instructions. Sammy was the only sober one present. He said to me, 'It's known throughout the world that I like a drink, but I have to stay sober. You know why I'm the only sober one here?'

'No.' I said.

'Because I have to keep my one eye on Peter.' I didn't know he only had one eye until he tapped his glass eye and said, 'Not this one, though.'

He also had another reason for keeping sober. In 1969, shortly after marrying a chorus girl, Altovise Gore, Davis had been rushed to hospital with suspected liver failure. Doctors gave him six months to live if he didn't quit drinking. Altovise was instrumental in helping him quit the booze.

It turned out that Ava had given him other instructions too. Or at least she had asked him if he would be open to me about the many things she and Lawford had told me, and had explained at some length her reasons why I, in all the world, should be the one to know these things.

Davis was surprisingly forthcoming, but it was a while before he really opened up. It developed from my asking him about things he would never have expected me to know, and he talked frankly and honestly.

He was also frank and honest when he finally suggested that I ought to leave the party, especially when a hooker made advances towards me. Apparently it was all on the house, but Davis, obviously remembering Ava's words that I should not be led astray in any way (I think she felt that she had the monopoly on leading me astray), insisted I leave there and then.

My next big surprise came when I was at Ava's home – probably no more than a week after the party – and Frank Sinatra called her on the phone. They talked for a bit, and then she said to me, 'Francis wants to talk to you.'

That was decidedly unnerving. I took the phone and said, 'Hello?'

'Ava tells me what a great kid you are.'

'Does she?'

'She tells me you've got a wife and she can't get you into bed.'

I guessed she hadn't told him what had gone on between us before I'd got married, so I just mumbled something to the effect that we were just friends.

'Anything you wanna say to me, kid?'

I didn't know what he meant, so I said, 'When are you going to make another movie?'

'Some day, kid, but I can't find a script that excites me.'

With audacity, I said, 'Why don't I write you a script, and you and Ava can make it into a movie.'

He laughed and said, 'Me and Ava in a movie? We'd kill each other.' When he had stopped laughing, he said a little more earnestly, 'I hear Ava's been telling you things you shouldn't know.' It turned out that she'd spoken to him previously and told him what had taken place, and they'd had a blazing row.

'What do you mean?' I asked as innocently as I could.

'About me and Marilyn and certain other people and what really happened.'

I said, 'Yes, she's told me.'

'And she got Peter Lawford to tell you, and Sammy.'

'Yes.'

'I got one thing to say to you, kid. Never, ever, tell anyone else what you know in my lifetime.'

Even though he was on the phone thousands of miles away, calling from God knows where, I trembled. 'No, I won't,' I promised.

His tone changed, and he said with good humour, 'May you live for ever – and may the last voice you hear be mine. Now put Ava back on.' I did.

After she had hung up, Ava said to me, 'Remember what Frank said. And remember that I'm telling you the same. I wanted you to know because you should know. You *have* to know. But it's all for your ears alone. Maybe, in time, when you're an old man and me and Frank and Peter are all dust, you might feel the time is right to let others know. That's up to you.'

In fact, she went on at some length about keeping quiet, but at the same time she told me that what I did with all that information in time to come was up to me – up to my own conscience. What I did do was to start writing copious notes about all that she had told me, all that Sammy had said, and all that Lawford had admitted. I hadn't a clue at that time what I was going to do with those notes, but as I was starting out as a journalist, it seemed the practical thing to do.

Later I looked for opportunities to write an article based on my notes and realised that there was so much information in them, there was enough to make a book. So I planned, many years ago, to write a full-scale biography of Frank Sinatra one day. I never did that biography because, over the years, it was done all too often. And I always felt somewhat gagged and unable to write what I have now written here.

Thanks to my job, it wasn't difficult to get to meet or interview people who'd known and worked with Sinatra over the years, and I learned how to ask the right questions to get answers that would corroborate, or at the very least help to illuminate, the secrets with which I had been entrusted. Then I just saved them up, never knowing for sure that I would ever have need of them.

I realised that, had Ava known I was to turn my hand to journalism in 1974, she would never have let me know all she told me – nor would she have made Lawford and Davis tell me. For years after, as our friendship began to disintegrate while my journalistic career progressed, she would say to me, often under the influence of drink, 'You'll write some goddamn story about me. "How I fucked Ava Gardner".'

I swore to her that I wouldn't.

Then she'd say that I'd write articles about Frank Sinatra and 'kick up all kinds of hell'. I promised her I wouldn't. And I kept my word.

So why did she tell me all this? Why did she get Peter Lawford and Sammy Davis Jr to talk to me about things they never talked to anybody else about? I can never know the answer for sure, but I think it had something to do with my young age, and her growing sense of mortality – for herself and others. It had something to do with somebody not of her generation having to know, first and foremost, what really happened to Marilyn Monroe – that was what really set off the bee in her bonnet. It also had something to do with someone, again not of her own generation, knowing that Frank Sinatra had done something – *really* done something – to make amends by finding some kind of redemption in an act the Sicilians call a 'vendetta'.

I just happened to be the person she chose, for whatever reasons she had. Perhaps it was just my own youthful exuberance and enthusiasm for that place of glamour and tinsel called Hollywood; a place she had escaped because she saw it all with the glamour and tinsel swept away. I questioned her over and over about Hollywood and the great stars she worked with, and she seemed hell bent on teaching me that Hollywood was not, and had never been, quite what I thought it was. She had seen it at its worst, and she wanted me to see it through her eyes.

She certainly never expected me to become a journalist and then an author and to end up writing this story. Yet she saw me as the future, that 'generation who needs to know', and I think she gained a certain kind of contentment from knowing that someone, in years to come, would be able to look back on the history of Hollywood, of crime and, indeed, a part of American history, and say, 'That's not the way I heard it.' In 1974 I seemed to have her full trust about such things. When I began my career as a journalist, however, I could tell that she regretted having been so open with me.

In 1974 Peter Lawford married his third and final wife, Patricia Seaton. By this time, however, he was a truly sick man. His deterioration continued, and he had to undergo emergency surgery for a bleeding ulcer.

In 1984 his friend of many years, Elizabeth Taylor, made an attempt to get Lawford back to work, and she also tried to help him get to grips with his alcoholism. It was not to be. The years of grief, fear and guilt had taken their toll, and towards the end of 1984 his ulcer finally burst and he went into a coma. He died on Christmas Eve.

Sinatra heard the news about Lawford's death while he was eating dinner. An observer said that Sinatra made the sign of the cross, said nothing, and went back to eating. It seemed to everyone that he hardly cared about the loss of his one-time friend, but I'm not convinced. I remember Ava telling me, 'Francis was furious with Peter only because he had told the FBI they should question him about Marilyn's death. That, to Francis, was pure stupidity. Not even Francis would hold a grudge against the messenger that tells him the president isn't coming to stay. But I have the feeling he always regretted losing a man who was such a good friend one time.'

If Frank Sinatra regretted losing his friend over 'stupidity', I cannot see him being anything but regretful over the terminal loss of that one-time friend.

Chapter Seventeen

Witnesses for Frank

In June 1975, Ava gave me the news that Frank was finally safe from exposure of his collaboration with the FBI. He was also safe from death on the orders of Sam Giancana. On 19 June, the day Giancana was to testify before the Senate Select Committee on Intelligence, Sam the Cigar was shot dead in the basement of his home. He had been shot once in the back of the head with a .29-calibre automatic, again in the mouth, and five times under the chin. It was a thorough and professional job.

Ava said, 'Francis certainly didn't shed a fucking tear over Giancana's death.'

It was, for Sinatra, a time of great triumph. He had spent the early summer of 1975 on a record-breaking tour of Europe, including Munich, Paris, Frankfurt and Vienna. He had come back from his so-called retirement to find himself still 'King of the Hill' and had agreed to play Caesar's Palace in Las Vegas (a place he had sworn never to play again after his fracas with Sanford Waterman). His opening night there on 19 June 1975 was a sensational success.

He stayed up late and went to bed in the early hours of the morning, sleeping right through until the afternoon of 20 June. When he awoke, he ordered breakfast from room service, and an omelette with basil-flavoured tomato sauce – his usual – was duly delivered. As he ate breakfast, he listened to the radio, and he heard the news that Giancana had been shot dead.

Ava told me, 'I asked Francis how he felt about the news, and he said, "Like I say, you live by the fucking sword, you die by the fucking sword." I very nearly reminded him that he had lived pretty damn close to the sword, but thought better of it. These days, I don't argue with Francis. He seemed kind of sombre, because, I suppose, Giancana had once been his friend. But there was no doubt he felt very satisfied indeed that it had all come to an end at last.'

Others who were around Sinatra at the time failed to note the sense of triumph and finality he must secretly have harboured. He was heard to say, 'Too goddamn bad for him.' Apart from that, he kept his real thoughts private from almost everybody.

Sinatra may not have shed tears for Giancana, but Eddie Fisher, his replacement as Sam's favourite entertainer, was distressed at the news. Whether or not Fisher ever figured out that he had been a sort of surrogate Sinatra for Giancana, he nevertheless compared their relationships to Sam the Cigar. He wrote, 'Sinatra always wanted to be a tough guy. I didn't; I just liked hanging around with tough guys.'

There were rumours that a faction of the Outfit itself had ordered the hit on Giancana because he had refused to share the immense wealth that he had amassed while in exile. Other rumours suggested that the CIA had had him killed to protect their own secrets. In fact, over the next several years, all the major players involved in the CIA/Mafia covert operations were carefully disposed of, including Johnny Roselli. In 1976 his body parts were found in a sealed oil drum floating off the coast of Florida.

It just so happened that, the first chance he got after hearing of Giancana's death, Frank tried to make contact with Johnny

Roselli. He left word everywhere that he wanted to talk to him, but for several weeks there was no sight nor sound of Roselli. Then, all of a sudden, in 1976, Frank got news from his secret intelligence source. Roselli was giving secret testimony to the Senate Select Committee on Intelligence, giving details about the CIA/Mafia efforts to invade Cuba and assassinate Fidel Castro. It was thought that he was also providing information about the assassination of President Kennedy.

This news was surprising enough in itself, but Frank was even more astonished when he suddenly got a phone call from Johnny Roselli.

'Where are you calling from?' Frank asked him.

'I can't say.'

'You sound a little scared, Johnny.'

'Frank, I never asked you a personal favour, did I?'

'No, I can't recall you ever did.'

'But I'm asking now. I need your help.'

'You in some kind of trouble, Johnny?' Frank was, said Ava, enjoying this moment.

'I'm not safe anywhere,' said Roselli.

'This got something to do with the killing of Sam the Cigar?' Frank realised he had Roselli by the nose, and he began asking questions, all the time making it seem like he would give Roselli the help he needed. He asked who had killed Sam? Roselli seemed unable to answer. Frank made a suggestion. 'Was it you?'

To this, all Roselli would say was, 'Santo'll have me killed.'

Frank knew he meant Santo Trafficante, and he knew well how Roselli and Trafficante had been making plenty of illicit money down in Florida together while the heat was on the Outfit in Chicago. Frank came up with his own scenario, suggesting that Santo had decided he didn't want Giancana saying anything that would blow his Florida operation, and had told Roselli to see to it that Sam never said anything to anyone – just like the time Sam had told Roselli to make sure Marilyn Monroe never said anything to anyone.

Roselli wouldn't respond. He just hung up. Frank knew he had pressed all the right buttons. He never heard from Roselli again, and he had no hand in Roselli's death. In fact, his death turned out to be just one of many that followed in the wake of the formation of the US House Select Committee on Assassinations – which, Sinatra learned from his FBI source, was a direct result of Roselli's testimony regarding the killing of Jack Kennedy. A number of prominent Mafia figures who appeared before the committee died suddenly, and some who were scheduled to appear died before they could do so. About the only one who didn't come to an untimely end was Santo Trafficante, who appeared before the committee but provided it with nothing useful whatsoever.

It was around this time that Ava stopped discussing Frank's life with me. I had established myself as a journalist, and she was increasingly wary of me as 'a goddamn reporter'. It became her quest to make me change my career and become an actor, and it was only when I didn't make an initial success as an actor but did as an author that she started to distance herself from me. I don't believe there was anything more of a confidential nature she could have told me anyway, with Sam Giancana dead and Frank getting on with his life and career.

Perhaps it was because he had put the past behind him by being a part of Giancana's downfall, as well as Roselli's, that in his latter years Frank Sinatra just continued to mellow. You couldn't count on that to think you could get one over on him, however. He could still be volatile, but age had certainly made him less likely to do anyone any real damage. He had also left behind, in so far as he could, all his Mob ties. Unfortunately, those ties were not easily broken.

In 1976 he performed at the Westchester Premiere Theater in

New York, a place that was said to have Mafia backing. After his first performance, Sinatra found he had visitors in his dressing room. They were Carlo Gambino (the biggest Mafia boss in America until his death a little later that year), Paul Castellano, Joseph Gambino and several other renowned mobsters.

They wanted their photograph taken with him and, unable to refuse them, he agreed. It became a classic picture, turning up in *Life* magazine in January 1979. As far as the world was concerned, Frank Sinatra was still rubbing shoulders with the Mafia.

After his divorce from Mia, Sinatra swore that he would never get married again. Yet he did, in July 1976, to Barbara Blakely Marx. They had been seeing each other since 1971, when Barbara was still married to Zeppo Marx. The Marxes had become very friendly with Sinatra and were often at his Palm Springs home for a game of cards or just to have dinner. In December 1972 Barbara filed for divorce, and shortly thereafter she moved into a condo close to Sinatra's house. It would seem that Sinatra's offspring, based on what Tina Sinatra later wrote, were far from enchanted by Barbara. But Frank was, and on 11 July 1976, Frank and Barbara were married.

In 1981, that photo of Frank with the Mafia leaders backstage at the Westchester came back to haunt him when he applied for a Nevada gambling licence. He was called to testify on 11 February 1981 in the city council chambers of Las Vegas. He brought with him character witnesses who included the Los Angeles county sheriff, Kirk Douglas and Gregory Peck.

Sinatra needed to prove that he was 'a person of good character, honesty and integrity, a person whose prior activities, criminal record, if any, reputation, habits and associations do not pose a threat to the public interest', according to the statute laid down in Nevada. This meant he had to prove he had no connections whatsoever to the Mafia.

As the Nevada Gaming Commission had no power to subpoena anyone, they were unable to call any known underworld figures to testify. This was Sinatra's great advantage. He could call witnesses of his own choosing who would only provide glowing testimonies regarding his many charitable works. It also helped, some observers noted, that Sinatra had changed his political allegiance from the Democrats to the Republicans and allied himself closely to President Ronald Reagan.

Ronald and Nancy Reagan's names were on the list of character witnesses Sinatra submitted to the Nevada board, knowing that the president would not be asked to appear personally. President Reagan did provide the board with a letter of recommendation, however, describing Sinatra as 'an honourable person, completely loyal and honest'.

When the Los Angeles sheriff was asked if he was aware of any connections Sinatra had with the Mafia, he had no compunction in stating, 'If Mr Sinatra is a member of the Mafia, then I'm the Godfather.'

Sinatra, understandably, was very nervous, and he hoped that his celebrity witnesses, Kirk Douglas and Gregory Peck, would deliver the goods.

When Kirk Douglas took the oath, he said, 'I don't know what the qualifications are to own a casino. And I want to be very careful in delineating Mr Sinatra's character. I must confess, I have found him guilty of professional jealousy.' That made Sinatra sit up with a scowl. Douglas continued, 'Oh yes. Years ago, I made a record of a song I sang in *20,000 Leagues Under the Sea*, called "A Whale of a Tale". And I felt that there was professional jealousy on his part!'

Everybody in the room laughed, and a relieved Sinatra smiled. Barbara later told Douglas, 'Thank God for you. You finally got a smile out of Frank, and relaxed him a bit.'

When Gregory Peck was called, he said that Frank Sinatra was 'one of the greatest artists in the popular field in our country... one of the finest men and the most honestly reliable, truthful man I personally have ever known'.

Hank Greenspun, publisher of the *Las Vegas Sun*, described an incident that had sparked the events leading to Sinatra's licence being revoked, when Frank and the late Ed Olsen, former chairman of the Nevada Gaming Board, had cross words on the subject in 1963. 'It was nothing more than a shouting match,' said Greenspun.

Sinatra's attorney, Mickey Rudin, gave his testimony and claimed that the FBI had been 'out to get' Frank. He said that many of the details in reports drawn up by J. Edgar Hoover were simply a mixture of rumour and innuendo. (Whether or not Mickey Rudin ever knew about his client's dealings with a faction of the FBI in regard to nailing Sam Giancana, I do not know.)

Rudin was questioned regarding an incident that had occurred at the Cal-Neva in 1963 when a fight broke out between the singer Phyllis McGuire and her road manager, Victor La Croix. Rudin was asked where Sinatra was on that night.

Rudin said that Sinatra had been 'back and forth several times' between Los Angeles and Nevada on that night.

Was Sinatra at the Cal-Neva when Giancana was there?

'I would have to tell you it was my recollection that he was not there, and I would have to tell you that I don't have that much confidence in my recollection. Maybe I fixed it in my mind that he wasn't there and that's now the story.'

Rudin said that he did know, however, that Frank did not invite Giancana to the Cal-Neva. 'Both of us were upset that he was there.' He said he couldn't remember exactly whether it was he or Sinatra who sent a message to Giancana to leave. 'But I do know that neither one of us invited him, and we were unhappy about his being there.'

When asked why Sinatra had voluntarily given up his gaming licence, Rudin responded by saying, 'Jack Warner said he wanted Sinatra out of Nevada and that his being in Nevada would be a problem for Warner [Bros].' At that time, Sinatra had been making a deal with Warners for a number of pictures, including one he would direct, *None but the Brave*.

Then came the time for Frank Sinatra to tell it his way. It was, to all intents, a performance, because, when asked about his Mafia associations, he had no choice but to be economical with the truth. He came completely prepared with documents, notes and legal records, giving a testimony that lasted five and a half hours.

He was asked, 'You never discussed with Mr Giancana the fact that you might be a front for him at the Cal-Neva, or that he might have some kind of hidden interest there?'

'No, never,' replied Sinatra.

He was asked about the visits made by Giancana to the Cal-Neva in 1963, which had led to his licence being revoked. Sinatra responded, 'I never invited Mr Giancana to the Cal-Neva Lodge. I never entertained him. And I never saw him.'

He was told that his testimony contradicted statements made by Phyllis McGuire – given on 27 January 1981, when she had said that Sam Giancana was at the Cal-Neva for the first few days that she and her singing sisters were engaged there, and that Sinatra *had* been present on that occasion because he had broken up a fight between McGuire and her road manager.

To this, Sinatra stated that he was in Los Angeles when the fight erupted. It was then pointed out to him that, in 1963, he had told Olsen that Giancana *was* at the Cal-Neva.

Frank replied, 'I might have said it. I was frustrated. I was angry. I might have said anything. But if I said it, I didn't mean it.'

He said that when he realised that Giancana was at the Cal-Neva one night in 1963, he thought he remembered Mickey Rudin telling Giancana to leave the premises.

In regard to the Villa Venice, Sinatra said that he was unaware of any connection between the Villa Venice and Sam Giancana. He said that Giancana had not asked him to perform there, but it was 'just possible' that he may have seen Giancana while performing there.

When asked how he had first met Giancana, Sinatra replied that he could not recall how and when they first met. He said, 'I never had anything to do with him business-wise and rarely, rarely, socially. No connection whatsoever.'

Frank was questioned about his trip to Havana in 1947, and he replied that he had not gone there to meet Lucky Luciano or any underworld figures, but had simply gone there 'to find sunshine'.

When it was suggested that he had gone to Havana carrying an attaché case containing two million dollars in cash, Frank answered, 'If you can find me an attaché case that holds two million dollars, I will give you the two million.'

He was asked why his name and address were found among Luciano's possessions during a search by Italian police. Sinatra said he had no idea.

When he was challenged with the suggestion that his early career was helped by the Mob, he replied, 'That's ridiculous.'

The photo of Sinatra and leading Mafia figures that had been published in *Life* was produced, and he was asked why he had been visited by a 'who's who and what's what in the area of organised crime'. Sinatra said that he had simply been told by one of the theatre employees that Mr Gambino was in the theatre with his granddaughter, whose name just happened to be Sinatra, and had asked if a photograph could be taken of the little girl with Frank. 'Before I realised what happened, there were approximately eight or nine men standing around me, and several other snapshots were made. I didn't even know their names, let alone their backgrounds.'

Knowing this photo would be used, he produced other photos of himself with Gregory Peck and the prime minister of Israel, with his wife Barbara and Anwar Sadat, and another with several men who looked like 'unsavoury guys' who just happened to be members of the San Francisco Police Department. 'If you look at this picture without my telling you this, it's frightening.'

The subject of the incident at Caesar's Palace, when Sanford Waterman had pulled a gun on Sinatra, was also raised. Sinatra explained that he had just come off stage and had gone to see Waterman and asked for credit. 'He gave me a rough time,' he said. 'I thought maybe he was going senile or something because he had never spoken to me like that before.' He said that Waterman put the gun to his ribs, and Frank told him, 'You're never gonna hurt me.' He said that he actually saved Waterman by whacking the gun from his hand and getting him into an office, because there were people around 'wanting to take his head off'.

Asked if he had been told to intercede with John or Bobby Kennedy on behalf of Giancana, Sinatra said he had never done that.

Sinatra was rewarded with his gaming licence. Despite that photograph of him with all the Mafia bosses at the Westchester Premiere Theater, the hearing did much to vindicate Frank. Perhaps he deserved that, because, after all, he was then a man trying to put his past behind him – and he had been instrumental in putting Sam Giancana out of action.

As for the glowing testimonies from Douglas and Peck, two men held in the highest esteem in the American film industry, they represented the way the industry viewed Frank Sinatra in his later, mellower years, with his Mob connections all but severed.

Perhaps the final connection was cut in 1982 when Skinny

D'Amato died from a heart attack. This was one underworld friend Sinatra was saddened to lose. D'Amato had been perhaps the only mobster who didn't try to use the favours he had shown Sinatra as a means of obligating him to a life of debt. D'Amato didn't need to insist on Sinatra's gratitude. He had simply earned it, and Frank was happy to give it. When D'Amato died, Frank grieved.

Chapter Eighteen

Hollywood Acceptance

Sinatra had been shrewd in asking both Kirk Douglas and Gregory Peck to testify on his behalf. Kirk Douglas had long been a friend of Frank Sinatra and must have known of his Mob associations, but he was not questioned about that particular subject before the gaming board in Las Vegas.

Although Douglas had known Frank for many years, he had never sought that friendship, nor did he, like some others, yearn to become one of Sinatra's cronies. In fact, he came to an interesting conclusion about why Frank Sinatra's closest friends had a tendency to find themselves suddenly excluded from his presence. 'There were always people who tried to get too close to Frank,' he said, 'and they were the ones who, for some unexplained reason that they could never figure out, were suddenly *out*. In fact, our home in Palm Springs became a halfway house for the people he tended to discard, even if temporarily.

'Even Greg and Veronique, who were really good friends of Frank's – Greg, as well as me, spoke up for him when he applied for his gaming licence – found themselves in that position once, and they spent several weekends at our halfway house before they were allowed to become a part of Frank's in-crowd again. The same thing happened to Pat DiCicco.' (DiCicco was, as

Douglas must have known, once a front man for Lucky Luciano in Hollywood and had married Thelma Todd, the actress Luciano killed.)

Kirk said he was convinced the reason that his friendship with Sinatra survived intact over many years was that he never tried to get close. He recalled that, when he was among a select group of guests gathered to celebrate Frank's eightieth birthday, he watched as Frank and Gregory Peck were engaged in an intense conversation. 'I don't ever remember talking with Frank for more than a minute or two at a time,' said Kirk. 'I figured that Greg really knew Frank, but I don't. My wife, Anne, got along better with him than I did. On one of her birthdays, Frank insisted on coming over to our house with all his cooking utensils and ingredients to make an Italian feast which he personally served. He would never have done that for me.'

Kirk once related a story to his wife Anne that he had heard, about a fistfight Sinatra had got into in Las Vegas. He said that it was when Frank was 'young and rambunctious'. Sinatra was performing in Las Vegas. After his act was over he went to the casino, where he exceeded his limit and was told he couldn't gamble any more. He demanded to see the owner, Carl Cohen, but was told that Mr Cohen was asleep. Frank started making a scene, so someone was sent to wake Cohen up. When he came down, he was faced with Sinatra yelling at him. Cohen punched him in the face and knocked out a couple of teeth.

Anne warned Kirk, 'Don't ever mention that story to Frank.'

'I already did. You know what Frank said? "I learned something, Kirk. Never fight a Jew in the desert."'

The story was actually one of the many Frank Sinatra urban myths. Others knew the story, and each had their own version of events, such as the singer Sonny King, who was there on the night of the fight in 1965. The hotel was the Sands, run by Carl Cohen. King's version had Frank turning up so drunk that he was refused credit. Sinatra found himself a golf cart, which was used by guests to get around the huge hotel, and drove it through the window of the hotel restaurant.

Cohen was called, and Sinatra told him, 'I'll tell you what I'm gonna do. I'm gonna punch you in the fucking mouth.'

He lunged at Cohen, who simply tipped over a table, which caught Sinatra off guard, and then hit him, breaking one of his front teeth. Frank was on his back, blood pouring from his mouth. He looked up at his bodyguard and said, 'Get him.'

Carl Cohen told the bodyguard, 'You make one move, they won't know which part of the desert to find you in.'

A variation on that same tale was told by Mia Farrow, to whom Frank was married at the time. She recalled what came to be 'one of those interminable Vegas nights'. She said that she and Frank were in a golf cart, returning to their part of the hotel. It was obviously sometime during daylight hours because he was wearing a shoebox on his head to keep the sunlight out of his eyes.

There had been some trouble at the casino, 'but things finally got smoothed over and nothing came of it'. As they were returning to their room in the golf cart, however, Frank suddenly pressed down on the gas pedal and drove straight towards a huge window. At the last minute he swerved and hit the window side on.

He jumped out of the cart and strode into the casino, threw some chairs into a heap and tried to set fire to them with his golden lighter. Mia just looked on in silence at 'the rising commotion as people gathered around and casino guards rushed over'.

When he couldn't get the fire started, Frank took Mia's hand and they just walked away.

As Kirk Douglas said, Gregory Peck had been a close friend of Sinatra's for many years. Peck had also been a great friend of Ava Gardner (Ava swore to me that Gregory Peck was one of the few leading men she never slept with). Peck and Ava had worked together on *The Snows of Kilimanjaro* and he was aware of the problems Sinatra had caused the location shooting by demanding that Ava work only ten days. In 1971, however, Peck discovered at first hand the charitable side of Sinatra.

Peck had a position on the board of the Motion Picture and Television Relief Fund, which ran the Country House and Hospital in Woodland Hills, where veterans of the industry could live in happy retirement. They needed an immediate injection of half a million dollars, so Peck produced the fiftieth-anniversary gala for the Fund at the Los Angeles Music Center in June 1971. All the celebrities Peck asked to take part agreed, including Sinatra, who had already announced his legendary (if temporary) retirement. He said that this would be his last performance before bowing out, and the result was a sell-out.

When Sinatra was announced as the 1972 recipient of the prestigious Scopus Award, given by various important Jewish organisations, Peck happily agreed to be the one to hand him the award. In 1978 Sinatra returned the compliment by handing Peck the Scopus Award. The singer Dinah Shore also received an award that year, and she, Peck and Sinatra were asked to pose for a photograph. For reasons I've never been able to discover, however, Sinatra lost his temper and, after letting out a string of abuse at the cameramen, he stormed out.

This may have been what Kirk Douglas had referred to when Gregory Peck was suddenly *persona non grata* at Sinatra's home. Whatever it was that had caused Sinatra's show of temper, it did not do any long-lasting damage to his friendship with Peck, and in 1981 Sinatra was able to persuade Peck to make a television commercial for Chrysler, for whom Frank was a volunteer spokesman. Sinatra personally gave Peck a guided tour of the Chrysler plant in Detroit and told him that the company was in trouble and that its 600,000 employees could find themselves out of work. Consequently, Peck agreed to do the commercial – and then donated his entire fee to the Motion Picture and Television Relief Fund.

There is no doubt that both Kirk Douglas and Gregory Peck spoke honestly before the Nevada Gaming Board by simply telling it just how they saw it. Sinatra had become known for his charitable work by the late 1970s and early 1980s, even though he had been serving charities for much longer. The shadow of the Mafia had loomed so large over him in those earlier days that it had overshadowed all the good he did.

No doubt, he could have called many others who would have spoken just as glowingly as Peck and Douglas. Yul Brynner might well have been one of the chosen few if it hadn't been for the fact that, by 1981, he was permanently touring the world in an ongoing stage revival of *The King and I*.

In the 1960s Yul Brynner had been one of Frank's closer friends. He was at Sinatra's Palm Springs home on many weekends. In 1979, he told me:

'Frank is a very complicated guy. But then, so am I. And so is Kirk [Douglas]. The three of us had made a film together, *Cast a Giant Shadow*, and we seemed to find something in common. I got on well with both Frank and Kirk. Kirk is an easy man to get on the wrong side of, and so is Frank – and so am I. So – we were ideal as friends and we were not ideal as friends.

'Both Frank and Kirk have wonderful homes – playing grounds – in Palm Springs, but I tended to spend more time with Frank because Kirk is a happily married man and Frank was, until he married Mia [Farrow], a fun-loving bachelor. I always knew I would have fun at his place.

'Now, remember, I said that we were all men that any one could fall foul of. With Kirk, I think it had something to do with his troubled childhood when his father was so tough on him. With me, it's all the different emotional and angry bloodlines coursing through my veins. With Frank, it was something to do with his

Sicilian and Italian origins, as well as a tendency to want to be a Mafia don. That's right! But by the time I became friends with Frank, he had left so much of that behind him.

'I guess there was one day when I wouldn't let Frank be Top Man because all of a sudden he was freezing me out. You know about his association with Sam the Cigar Man, right? Ava Gardner told you all about that? I remember Frank telling me, oh, round about 1965, that he was through with that gangster and that he never wanted anything to do with gangsters again. He said he'd put paid to Sam the Cigar Man. Did you know that? You probably know more than I do. He didn't talk of it much. I did say to him, "If you have put paid to Sam the Cigar Man, can you be sure he doesn't put paid to you?"

'He said, "Sam the Cigar is history, man. I've seen to it."

'I just said, "Oh, well you know best."

'He got quite angry with me about that. He didn't talk to me for a few weeks. So I didn't go to play at his house. I played at Kirk's house instead.

'He got over his little sulk, though. I said he was an easy man to upset. But he never got over being Top Man, and when you've got Kirk, Frank and me, we all want to be Top Man.

'Then one day Frank and I meet up and he says, "Where've you been? I missed you," and all of a sudden it's as though nothing happened, and I was vying with him to be Top Man again. We're still friends. But I have to pretend to let him be Top Man or he sulks!'

Another he could have called upon was Faye Dunaway, who, in late 1980, had much to thank Frank for. She had been filming *Mommy Dearest*, portraying Joan Crawford, and the many scenes that called for her to scream and shout took their toll on her vocal chords. Afraid that she might have actually damaged her vocal chords, she called Frank, with whom she had previously worked on what was essentially Sinatra's comeback movie, *The First*

Deadly Sin. (The film had taken some years to reach fruition, planned originally in the late seventies as a vehicle for Roman Polanski to direct, with Marlon Brando starring as a detective nearing retirement with one murder case to crack while his wife lies dying from an incurable illness. In 1977 Polanski fled America with a statutory rape charge hanging over him, and Brando lost interest in the project. Sinatra saw the opportunity to make his movie comeback, having tested the water in 1977 with a telemovie, *Contract on Cherry Street*, and with him on board in Brando's role of the detective, filming started in January 1980 and finished in March, and the movie was released in October – to disastrous reviews and box office sales. After that, Frank gave up movies, except for a brief guest appearance in *Cannonball Run II* in 1984.)

Faye Dunaway felt that, if anyone could help her with her vocal problems, Frank could and would. She recalled how, in their scenes together in *The First Deadly Sin*, 'Frank treated me with real respect.' That was a long way from how he'd treated some of his former leading ladies of the fifties, such as Shelley Winters: an indication of just how much he had mellowed.

Fay remembered Frank taking her and others to a casino in Atlantic City, 'where he was truly in his element'. They stayed up all night while Frank talked about his life in Hollywood, and about Ava Gardner. He talked about 'how people would just stop in their tracks when she passed and turn around and stare at her. She was just this truly *beautiful* woman.' In 1980 Frank still had incredibly strong feelings for Ava. Faye said it was 'one of the most memorable evenings I had ever had. I loved talking to this wonderful artist.'

So when her voice went, Faye didn't hesitate to call Frank and tell him her problem. He gave her the name of a throat specialist he had used, and the very next day he drove from Palm Springs to her home in Los Angeles to teach her the tricks he used to save his own vocal chords. With his help, she got her voice back.

Ingrid Bergman was another who could have given the gaming board a glowing reference. She could easily have told them how, in November 1979, Frank stepped in to help when she was invited by the Variety Club of America to be guest of honour at a television special to raise funds to build an Ingrid Bergman wing for underprivileged and handicapped children.

She had never worked with Frank and hardly knew him, but when he heard about the tribute, he called the show's producer Mike Frankovich and said, 'I want to be a part of Ingrid's tribute because I've always wanted to sing "As Time Goes By" to her.'

As Ingrid Bergman recalled, 'He was opening his own show in Atlantic City the very next night, but he flew three thousand miles to attend our show, sing one song, and fly straight back again. I was very touched by his generous nature.'

It was that generous nature that was finally helping to overshadow Frank's shady past – but it didn't blot all of it out. There were many who never forgave him. Shelley Winters was among those who did. Despite all the brouhaha that ensued when they made *Meet Danny Wilson* in 1952, by 1981 they were friends again. 'During the last ten years,' she said, 'Frank always invites me to his openings at Caesar's Palace, and I always go.'

Lee Marvin was also one to forgive and forget, despite having once squared up to Sinatra during the days when they were both tough guys. When Lee married Pamela Feeley in 1970, Sinatra stepped in to help. Marvin told me:

'I'd just got through that goddamn affair with Michelle [Triola] and decided that if I was going to be a married man, there was no one I wanted to marry more than Pamela whom I'd known for twenty-five years. I got on the phone to [PR man] Jim Mahoney and told him that I wanted to get this wedding done fast and I didn't want anyone to know about it until it's all done. He said, "Where are you getting married?"

'I said, "Vegas."'

'So Pamela and I flew from New York to Los Angeles, where I had my house in Malibu. It turned out that Mahoney had got onto another client of his who happened to be Frank Sinatra, and he told him I needed to get to Vegas quickly. Frank simply said, "They can have my plane."'

'Now me and Pamela knew nothing about this. We left our house, all dressed for the ceremony, and drove to Clovefield Airport, and we got there where Jim Mahoney and his wife met us. Then, VAROOOOM, this big DeHavilland roars in, and Jim says, "Frank Sinatra sends his plane as a wedding gift." So we climbed aboard and we were in Vegas and married before anyone in the press knew about it.

'Now that was a really nice thing Frank did for us, considering we didn't exactly hit it off at the beginning. But that's Frank: if he can help, he just has an impulse to do it, and if I didn't tell you this now, nobody would ever know about it, because he doesn't do it for the publicity.

'Most people I've known for years in the business remain pretty much who they were and are – but Frank, he's someone who can start out as your worst enemy, but years later, he's your best friend just when you need him.'

It was that side to Sinatra's nature that even won over the most conservative of all Hollywood stars, John Wayne.

I spent some time with Wayne when he was in London in 1974 making *Brannigan*. I knew a bit about the background to how he and Kirk Douglas became involved in *Cast a Giant Shadow*, and the subject of Frank Sinatra came up. 'For a long time Frank and I never got along, not just because he's such a goddam liberal,' said Wayne, 'but because he always thought he was a gangster. I mean, he was a goddamn gangster! That's a side of him I just couldn't stand.'

I suggested to Wayne that he was aware, then, of Sinatra's Mob associations. 'Aware?' he said. 'Hell, who the hell doesn't know he's in with the Mafia?'

I did think of trying to explain how Sinatra had been turning that side of his life around, but thought better of it. Wayne talked of a time in 1960 when Sinatra had hired the screenwriter Albert Maltz, one of the infamous 'Hollywood Ten' who had been blacklisted by the Communist witch hunt, of which Wayne himself had been one of the leading lights. Sinatra wanted to make a film called *The Execution of Private Slovik* based on a book by William Bradford Huie. Wayne disliked the way the book portrayed the US military as the heavies, telling the story of the only American to be executed as a deserter during the Second World War.

Maltz and Sinatra had been friends since the Second World War, when Maltz wrote the screenplay for a short film called *The House I Live In*, which starred Frank. The mistake Sinatra made in 1960 was to announce Maltz as his screenwriter in advance of filming, unlike the case of another blacklisted writer, Dalton Trumbo, who was hired by Kirk Douglas to write *Spartacus*. Douglas had the good sense to wait until the film was in production before announcing that Trumbo was his screenwriter, and so break the blacklist for the first time. Sinatra, however, publicly announced the name of his writer long before filming commenced, or before his treatment could be turned into a screenplay.

Despite the subject of the story, Maltz actually gave the treatment a pro-American approach, which Sinatra personally praised. He was, after all, a patriot. But not everyone saw it that way.

'When I heard about it,' said Wayne, 'I was so goddamn mad, I told a reporter, "I wonder how Sinatra's crony, Senator John Kennedy, feels about Sinatra hiring such a man." The whole thing became a minefield, especially when Hedda Hooper attacked him in her column – so did the Hearst Press. I heard that Kennedy put pressure on Frank, and he had to back down. And he sure as hell didn't like it. He ended up paying Maltz 75,000 dollars *not* to write the goddamn thing.'

Sinatra had publicly announced, 'The American public has indicated it feels the morality of hiring Albert Maltz is the more crucial matter than his pro-American approach to the story, and I will accept this majority opinion.' (In the end, the episode portraying the execution was used, without reference to the actual fact, by the writer-director Carl Foreman, who had also been blacklisted, in his anti-war epic *The Victors*.)

Wayne told me, 'The next time I saw Frank was at a charity benefit, and he'd been drinking heavily. He walked up to me – and he's not exactly tall enough to see eye to eye with me – and he said, "You seem to disagree with me." I told him, "Just take it easy, Frank. We can talk about this later." And he said, "I want to talk about it right *now*." It's a good thing some of his friends pulled him away because I'd sure hate to have flattened him.'

The rift between Wayne and Sinatra suddenly vanished when, in 1976, the Variety Club produced a show in tribute to Wayne, who accepted the honour only when it was explained to him that the funds raised would go towards a children's ward named after him. To his great surprise, Frank Sinatra insisted on hosting the show in honour of the Duke, and Ol' Blue Eyes took the opportunity to sing to him, 'You Are the Sunshine of My Life'. Sinatra even allowed himself to become the butt of one of Wayne's best jokes of the evening, when, following tributes from such stars as James Stewart, Angie Dickinson, Maureen O'Hara and Lee Marvin, Wayne got up and said, 'Tonight you've made an old man and an actor very happy. You are happy, aren't you, Frank?'

Sinatra never intended to put himself in favour with John Wayne, but he did just that when he showed his support for the ultra-conservative Ronald Reagan in his bid for the presidency. Then, in 1979, when Wayne was dying from cancer, he made his final appearance at that year's Oscars ceremony. He knew it was his final public appearance. Frank Sinatra was there too, along with Sammy Davis, and each of them gave Wayne a big hug of true affection, never realising that their hugs caused the once seemingly indestructible but now frail John Wayne excruciating pain.

When Wayne was close to death in hospital, Frank Sinatra was one of the few non-relations permitted to visit him. If John Wayne could accept the one-time friend of many mafiosi as one of his own best friends in his dying days, then that said everything about Hollywood's acceptance of Frank Sinatra in his latter days.

Chapter Nineteen

A Life Turned Around

The heady days of the Summit's antics were over, but Sinatra, Martin and Sammy Davis remained firm friends, even if they didn't perform together quite so often. Joey Bishop seemed to fade purposely into the background, for reasons best known to himself.

Davis and Martin were reunited on screen in 1980 in *The Cannonball Run*, and were back for the sequel, unimaginatively titled *The Cannonball Run II*. This time, though, they were joined briefly by the Chairman of the Board himself. Sinatra agreed to appear at the behest of the director Hal Needham, who saw the gathering of the Summit in one film again as a considerable coup.

Typically, Sinatra arrived on the set in Old Tucson, Arizona, in his private jet and did his stint in just a single day.

Dom DeLuise, who co-starred in both pictures with Burt Reynolds, recalled, 'It was like the pope coming. Sinatra is the royalty in this business. But he is very patient. He must have posed for a thousand pictures with people. It's funny about a king like that. He doesn't know he's intimidating. He was sitting in a chair – we were all having our picture taken – and I mentioned that it would be good if he could stand with us, so we could all be together. But Burt turned aside and said, "Yeah, but who's going to tell him?" In the end, I told him.'

In 1985, I asked Ava if I could write about the reasons behind her difficult behaviour on the set of *55 Days at Peking* in my biography of Charlton Heston. I simply felt she ought to have the opportunity to answer the criticisms Heston had made of her (unaware as he was of the circumstances), but she forbade me to make any mention of it. In fact, she forbade me even to mention her name in the book, which was impossible for me to comply with, considering that she made two films with Heston. She was, of course, perfectly right in declining my offer, as any justification of herself would have blown the lid on what was a strictly no-go area. I therefore refrained from writing about it, and the published outcome did nothing to change Ava's reputation as a difficult actress.

When I wrote *The Hollywood Murder Casebook* in 1986, I asked Ava if I could, at the very least, suggest theories based on what she, Lawford and Sammy Davis had told me regarding the death of Marilyn Monroe. She told me, 'You write that stuff and I'll never fucking speak to you again.' So I had to write about Marilyn Monroe's murder without so much as a mention of Frank Sinatra, nor any of the things I'd been told. I was as good as my word. But she never did speak to me again.

During the 1980s, Frank Sinatra seemed a contented man, married to Barbara, who was with him to the end. In 1988 he opened the doors of his Palm Springs mansion for a Magic Carpet Weekend to raise cash for Barbara's centre for sexually abused children at the nearby Eisenhower Hospital. Guests willingly paid thousands of dollars each to be Sinatra's guests for the day.

By the time of Frank's eightieth-birthday party in December

1995, he was as much a part of the Hollywood establishment as any of his peers. Even Kirk Douglas, who had always avoided getting too close to Frank, allowed himself to get a little closer than he had ever done before. Kirk was at the bar when Frank joined him and ordered a Jack Daniel's.

'Spartacus,' said Frank, 'I like standing at a bar. Reminds me of when I was a kid – eleven or twelve years old – trying to reach up to my father's bar.'

Kirk said that this took him by surprise, because he had always thought Frank's father was a fireman. Kirk was obviously unaware of Frank's parents' involvement in the Mob-sponsored bar business.

Frank told Douglas that his parents had had 'a coin machine to play music' which he used to sing along to. 'They started giving me nickels, dimes and quarters, and I thought, hey, for singing? This is quite a racket.'

Kirk, whose father had been something of a neglectful brute, told Frank, 'I envy you. My father spent a lot of time in bars, but he never took me along.'

That, said Kirk, was the most personal conversation he and Sinatra had ever had. Then he raised his glass and said, 'Frank, happy birthday. Tonight, when you're lying in your bed, forget all the adulation and bouquets tossed at you this week. Just think what you've done since you left Hoboken, and give yourself a pat on the back. But make sure you thank God for the great talent that he gave you, and thank him for allowing you to use it in a way that has made a difference in the world.'

Kirk said that he thought Frank was touched, 'but you never knew what Frank was thinking'.

Whether or not Douglas knew it, he and Sinatra differed in opinion with regard to the existence of God. In his ageing years, Douglas had found his God while searching for his own roots as a Jew. Sinatra, although a Catholic by birth, never claimed to believe in a spiritual being. Maybe he just hoped there wasn't one, so he wouldn't be in too much trouble when his end came.

After dinner, Douglas and Sinatra walked out onto the covered veranda. A soft drizzle fell, and Frank gave Kirk an impish grin. For once, Douglas knew what he was thinking, and they both stepped out to look up at the sky and let the rain wash down their faces. 'That's the closest I ever got to Frank,' said Kirk.

Tina Sinatra wrote in her memoir that although many years had passed since Ava and Frank had divorced, never a week went by without some form of contact between them: 'Their tender affection was conveyed through funny notes and gifts, and routine phone calls.' Whenever Ava was in New York, she stayed at Sinatra's apartment, sometimes sharing it with Tina. The last time Tina saw Ava was at her Enismore Gardens flat in London, probably in 1989, when Tina noted that Ava's beauty had faded 'but not her feelings for my father'. Tina said she knew that Ava still loved him, and that the 'adoration was thoroughly mutual'.

When Ava fell ill, Frank was kept informed of her decline until, when she was too ill even to speak, he flew her to Los Angeles to see a specialist. When word reached him that she had died, on 25 January 1990, Frank remained alone in his room, seeing no one, speaking to no one. Tina tried to reach him by phone a number of times, but always Barbara would answer and tell her that he was still in his room. When she finally got to speak to him, 'he was distraught, barely audible'.

Ava died just after her autobiography was published. I was disappointed – but also relieved – to find that there was not one mention of me in it. I think by then she had blanked me out of her life.

Sammy Davis Jr also died in 1990, going just four months after Ava. He had been suffering with cancer of the throat and knew his days were numbered, yet the year before he died he joined

Sinatra and Liza Minnelli for a series of sell-out shows. (Dean Martin was to have been with them, but he was too sick and his place was taken by Liza Minnelli.) While in London in 1989, Sammy said, 'You name it and I've done it. I'd like to say I did it my way, but that line, I'm afraid, belongs to someone else.'

He could have had an operation to save his life, but he decided against surgery because his voice would have been lost for ever. He said, 'If I can't sing, I'd rather die.'

Still grieving over Ava's death, Frank had now lost Sammy, and his funeral was the last one Sinatra ever attended. He could not bring himself even to say goodbye formally to Dean Martin when he died on Christmas morning of 1995. He wanted to, but as he was dressing for the funeral, he broke down. Family members agreed that it would be best if he stayed away, so Barbara represented him at the funeral.

He did manage, however, to release a public statement to fend off the cynics who would take delight in declaring that Frank had snubbed Dino at the very end. He said, 'Too many times I've been asked to say something about friends who are gone. This is one of the hardest. Dean was my brother – not through blood but through choice. Our friendship has travelled down many roads over the years, and there will always be a special place in my heart and soul for Dean. He has been like the air that I breathe – always there, always close by.'

The 1990s were a depressing time for Sinatra. He could not come to terms with his own advancing years, or with losing the many people he had so loved. I wonder how often he might have reflected privately on his life and on the reasons why he had waged his vendetta against Sam Giancana. Did he ever consider telling anyone the whole truth? Indeed, did he actually get around to doing that? I have no way of knowing.

When I came to write *The Hollywood Connection* in 1991, which told the story of how the Mafia infiltrated Hollywood, Ava had been dead a year, but Frank Sinatra was still with us – and I wasn't about to cross him by writing all that I have done here. Most of all, however, I did not want to put him in a position of having to defend himself by forcing him to deny how he had uncovered the conspiracy over Monroe's death and had taken subsequent action. The only other option he could have taken was to admit to it, and that, I am quite certain, was altogether out of the question. So I was very careful about what I included in that book.

In 1971 Sinatra had famously retired, only to come out of retirement a few years later. He had always believed in his father's maxim, which he'd cited when he gave up prizefighting: 'You gotta get out before you hit the mat,' and so Frank had retired. Yet he had to come back again simply because, as Tina Sinatra saw it, 'the audience was where he lived.'

It was during the 1990s that, perhaps, he really should have retired. Instead, he simply worked more and more. There was probably no other time in his career when he was performing more live shows, and yet both his eyesight and his hearing were failing. In 1993 he had cataracts removed, but the improvement to his sight was minimal. He gave up painting, which he had enjoyed as a passionate hobby for fifty-odd years. He found it difficult to read, even with a magnifying glass, so he no longer read the newspapers avidly. His reason for working himself so hard at this time of his life was based on a simple philosophy he shared with many of his friends: 'If I stop working, I know I'll be next.'

In November 1996, Frank suffered a major heart attack. He recovered, but he was never the same again. Doctors discovered that he had, in fact, suffered a number of minor strokes prior to the heart attack. He also had ureter cancer, which was treated, but it returned in early 1998. A few months later, on 14 May, he suffered a fatal heart attack.

Now Sinatra is gone, and I've used my own conscience to

reveal what I know, because I think it is right that people should know. During his lifetime, Sinatra endured constant criticism for his way of life. Yet he did some heroic things – and he did them because they were right to do.

As I began to write this book, I was performing in a play, Arthur Miller's *A View from the Bridge*. I played the Italian-American lawyer Alfieri, who lives and works in New York, and as I uttered some of his lines, I was constantly reminded of Frank Sinatra.

'He was as good as he had to be,' was one line. Frank Sinatra is perceived by too many people as an entertainer who wanted to be a hood. That may have been true to a large extent, but when he realised that there were some mistakes he could try to rectify, he certainly did try.

Alfieri also spoke of the days when 'Al Capone, the greatest Carthaginian of all, was learning his trade on these pavements. Oh, there were many here who were justly shot by unjust men. Justice is very important here.'

Justice is what Frank Sinatra sought, having been brought up in an era when justice was more important to certain types than the law. To the Sicilians and the Italians, that is 'vendetta'.

'And now we are civilised, quite American. Now we settle for half, and I like it better.' The 'half' that was settled for was to allow the law to deal with justice, and surely that is what Sinatra ended up doing – in his own way.

Although Sinatra never confided in too many people about his vendetta, he nevertheless let it be known – and now more people than ever will know. As Alfieri said, 'But the truth is holy, and even as I know how wrong he was, I tremble, for I confess that something perversely pure calls to me from his memory – not purely good, but *himself* purely. For he allowed himself to be wholly known.'

Each night, as I uttered Alfieri's final line, I was constantly in mind of Sinatra – and of his still recent death. 'And yet, it is better to settle for half, it must be! And so I mourn him – I admit it – with a certain ... alarm.'

In my eyes, despite all his arrogance and temperament, especially in his earlier years, Sinatra was, in the end, a flawed hero who beat the Mafia at their own game, and turned his life around.

Selected Bibliography
and Sources

My first-hand sources were Ava Gardner, Peter Lawford, Sammy Davis Jr, John Huston, John Sturges, Stanley Kramer, John Frankenheimer, Burt Lancaster, Kirk Douglas, Tony Curtis, Natalie Wood, Lee Marvin, Gig Young, Shelley Winters, Melville Shavelson, Robert Mitchum, Lauren Bacall, Yul Brynner, David Niven, Robert Aldrich, Rex Harrison, John Wayne, Ingrid Bergman, James Brolin, John Leyton – and, of course, there was a word or two from the Chairman of the Board himself.

I resorted to researching as few books as possible, despite the many biographies of the subject, because, as I have stated, this was never intended to be a full-scale biography. The books listed below, few as they are, were useful in terms of helping me to place the events that I already knew about within the general history of the subject, as well as offering extra insight into the stories told to me first-hand by those I had got to know or formally interview during my years as a journalist, publicist and researcher.

Blakey, G Robert, and Richard H Billings. *The Plot to Kill the President*. Times Books, 1981.
Davis Jr, Sammy, with Jane and Burt Boyar. *Why Me*? Viking Penguin Inc., 1989
Douglas, Kirk. *Climbing the Mountain*. Simon & Schuster, 1997.

Dunaway, Faye, with Betsy Sharkey. *Looking For Gatsby: My Life*. HarperCollins, 1995.

Farrow, Mia. *What Falls Away*. Doubleday, 1997.

Fisher, Eddie. *Been There, Done That*. St Martin's Press, 1999.

Giancana, Sam and Chuck. *Double Cross*. Warner Books, 1992.

Hurt, Henner. *Reasonable Doubt*. Holt, Rinehart and Winston, 1985.

Heymann, C David. *R.F.K., A Candid Biography*. William Heinemann, 1998.

Kelly, Kitty. *His Way*. Bantam Books, 1986.

Sinatra, Tina. *My Father's Daughter*. Simon & Schuster, 2000.

Sterling, Claire. *The Mafia: The Long Reach of the International Sicilian Mafia*. Hamish Hamilton and Penguin, 1990.

Taraborrelli, J Randall. *Sinatra, the man behind the myth*. Rose Books, 1997.

Teresa, Vincent, with Thomas C Renner. *My Life in the Mafia*. Hart-Davis, McGibbon (UK), 1973.

Woolf, Marvin J, and Katherine Moder. *L.A. Crime*. Facts on File Publications, 1986.

Index